THE ULTIMATE REBOOT

Mastering Forgiveness, Gratitude and
Manifestation through Chakra Healing

KOUTILYA CHHAJED

Om Books International

First published in 2025 by

Om Books International

Corporate & Editorial Office
A-12, Sector 64, Noida 201 301
Uttar Pradesh, India
Phone: +91 120 477 4100
Email: editorial@ombooks.com
Website: www.ombooksinternational.com

Sales Office
107, Ansari Road, Darya Ganj,
New Delhi 110 002, India
Phone: +91 11 4000 9000
Email: sales@ombooks.com
Website: www.ombooks.com

ISBN: 978-93-6395-679-7

Printed in India

10 9 8 7 6 5 4 3 2 1

Koutilya Chhajed is a psychologist, integrative health practitioner and life coach with over two decades of experience in mental health, holistic healing and personal transformation. As the founder of Divibe Healing, he combines evidence-based psychological therapies with ancient wisdom practices such as chakra healing, mindfulness, yoga and energy work to support emotional well-being and spiritual growth.

Over the years, Koutilya has empowered thousands of individuals, families and organizations to overcome challenges like anxiety, depression, stress, relationship conflicts and behavioural struggles. His unique approach integrates Cognitive Behavioral Therapy, Narrative Therapy, and other validated methods with spiritual tools, helping clients move beyond limiting beliefs towards resilience, clarity and self-mastery.

His expertise spans corporate training, wellness coaching and psychotherapy, where he has worked with professionals, students and communities across India. Koutilya holds a master's in clinical psychology and multiple certifications in yoga, energy healing, hypnosis and well-being from esteemed institutions.

You can reach him on Instagram @divibehealing.

I am deeply grateful to my parents, family and friends,
whose love and unwavering support have been the anchor of my life.
To have you as my companions on this journey is a blessing beyond
measure.

To my clients, colleagues and workshop participants—
your trust has been both my inspiration and my teacher,
reminding me that every soul carries within it the courage to heal.

To those who doubted—
thank you, for your scepticism became the spark
that urged me to rise higher than I ever thought I could.

And to the universe—
with its quiet orchestration, weaving unseen threads of grace,
transforming distant dreams into living reality,
I bow in endless gratitude.

Contents

WEEK 1

Introduction

"Change is not something that we should fear. Rather, it is something that we should welcome. For without change, nothing in this world would ever grow or blossom, and no one in this world would ever move forward to become the person they're meant to be."
—B.K.S. Iyengar

Welcome to the 21-day ultimate reboot, a transformative journey towards harmony and alignment of your mind, body and soul. This journey about discovering balance through mental clarity and chakra renewal is designed to help you let go of stress and realign your energy. The book is a reliable, accessible guide for those moments when life feels overwhelming and your energy needs a reset.

Many of my clients and workshop attendees have often asked, "Is there a book I can turn to when I feel out of balance or stressed, a kind of self-healing manual?" This book is my answer to that. *The Ultimate Reboot* serves as your lifelong companion, whom you can rely on anytime you feel stuck, experience mental challenges or sense that a chakra is blocked. You can revisit these practices whenever you need to reconnect with your inner strength.

This is not a one-time journey—you can start this 21-day reboot anytime, as many times as you like. And if you ever feel stuck, confused or overwhelmed, simply open the book to a random page and try that exercise. Sometimes the universe has a way of guiding you exactly where you need to be, and the page you open could hold the answer you have been searching for or the solution you need to move forward.

Each day, you will be introduced to practices combining mental and energy healing, helping you release what no longer serves you. Remember, this is more than just a 21-day journey; it is a lifelong guide for renewal and growth. As you progress, you will find yourself more aligned, empowered and ready to embrace a vibrant, fulfilling life.

1 How to Get the Most Out of This Book

"If you have the ability to love, love yourself first."
—Charles Bukowski

Are you ready to transform your life into one filled with joy, purpose and connection? This 21-day ultimate reboot for your mind, body and soul is designed to help you release the weight of the past by forgiving others and yourself, live fully in the present by living in gratitude and start creating a future by manifesting your truest desires.

In this journey of transformation, you will get an opportunity to understand your mind, your emotions and how they impact every aspect of your life. It uses a unique blend of mental health detox and chakra healing to gently guide you towards happiness and well-being.

Before you dive in, try to absorb the concepts. Don't just rush through the exercises. It is not a checklist; it is a personal, intimate dance with your inner self. It is about understanding, not just doing.

And remember, consistency is your secret weapon. Try your best to complete these 21 days without stopping. It is only then you will experience the transformative power of this journey.

Think of this book as your personal diary, your safe space. Use the worksheets to write down your thoughts, your fears, your hopes. It is for your eyes only, a mirror reflecting your unique transformation.

Nourishing your body is an important part of this journey. For the next 21 days, pay attention to what you put into your body. Consider making choices that support your well-being—like opting for lighter, simpler meals and avoiding habits that might make you feel weighed down. These small changes can help clear your mind and bring a greater sense of emotional stability. It is all about creating a space that supports your overall well-being.

This is not a one-time thing. Feel free to revisit this journey every few months or at least once a year. Because each time, you will gain deeper insights and reinforce the changes you have made. It is like watering your garden of self-love.

Keep a close eye on your progress. Notice how you feel, how your thoughts are shifting. This will remind you of how far you have come, how much you have grown. It is a beautiful reminder of your strength and resilience.

Every day will become an opportunity to connect with the amazing person you are. You will discover a strength you never knew you had. You will learn to truly love and accept yourself.

Don't be afraid to share your experience with others. Their support can be a powerful source of encouragement.

And celebrate every tiny victory. Every step, no matter how small, brings you closer to the happiest version of you. You are worthy of this joy, this connection, this beautiful life.

Trust the process, be kind to yourself and enjoy this journey of transformation. You deserve this incredible gift of well-being.

2 ⸱⸱⸱|⸱⸱⸱ Reclaim Your Life's Narrative

"Life isn't about finding yourself. Life is about creating yourself."
—George Bernard Shaw

Have you ever found yourself wondering, *Why am I here?* or *What am I doing with my life?* These questions can swirl around in your mind endlessly. Did you know that the answers you are desperately seeking outside are actually hidden within you?

Yes, you read that right.

You possess incredible power, a strength that is uniquely yours. You just haven't fully realized it yet. We are our own harshest critics. We underestimate ourselves, our potential, our ability to create the life we truly desire. Trust me, the universe doesn't judge us, it doesn't criticize.

Embrace life's lessons

Life can be challenging, but we often make it more complicated than it needs to be. Too often, we create unnecessary struggles by our thoughts and choices. By clinging to the past, we trap ourselves in cycles of pain and regret, preventing us from fully embracing the beauty of the present.

We all have those moments when we wish we could hit the reset button—erase the past and begin again. But does life really work that way? No matter how much we want to, we can't go back and change what has already happened. So, why revisit it, why relive the hurt and pain all over again? Why keep asking, *Why did I do that?* or *I should have made a different decision?*

By clinging to these thoughts, you only deepen your own wounds. Each time you replay those memories, you chip away at your happiness in the present and your confidence about the future. These patterns erode your trust, not just in others, but in yourself.

You might be thinking, *It's easier said than done.* And you are right; it takes courage to let go. But look around you. Look at the successful people in this world. Do they dwell in their past? If they did, would they have created such beautiful futures for themselves? If your mind is stuck in yesterday, how can you truly enjoy today? And if you can't fully embrace the present moment, how can you design a happy future? It is a continuous loop, and you are the only one who can break free from it.

> "True forgiveness is when you can say, 'Thank you for that experience.'"—Oprah Winfrey

This doesn't mean forgetting your past entirely. No, it is about learning from it, growing from it and transforming yourself so you don't repeat those same mistakes. But there are decisions we make that can't be undone. So, what can you do now?

Transition from regret to renewal

First, let go of the regrets. What is done is done, and it is now part of your story. It is in the past. Own your mistakes although they don't define who you are, they help shape who you are becoming. Accept them as part of your journey. True strength lies in facing the consequences with courage and choosing to move forward.

"Forget regret, or life is yours to miss."—Jonathan Larson

Remember, you are your own best advocate. Take that first step, and you will discover the strength to keep going. The path to healing and growth starts with you. It is all in your hands.

Once you have embraced this mindset, start by actively looking for the good in every situation. It might sound simple—maybe even naive in tough times—but trust me, it is one of the most powerful tools you can use. If you lose your job, instead of focusing on the disappointment, try to see it as an opportunity. It could be a chance to explore your passions, to rediscover talents you never knew you had.

And what about losing someone? Losing a loved one is incredibly painful. If you are walking through that pain right now, know that my heart goes out to you. Try to find comfort in the thought that their suffering may be over. Perhaps they have finally found peace. Wouldn't you want that for them?

If you find yourself in a difficult relationship, one that feels like a cage you can't escape, I truly empathize with how hard that can be. It is important to ask yourself, *What's keeping me in this situation?* If you have chosen to stay, try to accept the reality of where you are right now. Let go of some unrealistic expectations, shift your perspective and try to focus on the qualities you appreciate in that person. It is not about accepting bad behaviour—it is about finding a way to cultivate your own peace and happiness, no matter the circumstances.

Be aware of the alchemy of thought

> "The world we have created is a product of our thinking."—Albert Einstein

As you shift your way of thinking, the world around you begins to change, creating a reality shaped by your thoughts. The Law of Attraction is real—what you give is what you get. It defines your ability to attract, into your life, what you focus on. And this "law" applies to all areas of life including health, finances and relationships. Life is a constant exchange. When you focus on the negative, you invite more negativity into your life. This cycle can easily entangle you, but here is the good news—you can break free by changing your mindset. It will not happen overnight, but every journey begins with that first step. Take it, and you will start to notice and feel the change.

As part of this journey, we will explore a practice called mental detox—a way to clear the clutter from your mind, helping you reconnect with your true purpose.

Remember, you can only build a future when you release the past and learn from it. Embrace the present and be grateful for everything, big or small. Your present moment is what defines your future. So, make your present moment one of gratitude and joy. When it becomes your past, you will have beautiful memories to hold on to. This gratitude creates a cycle of positivity, hope and endless possibility.

Heal and realign

In this journey, we will also explore chakra healing—a powerful practice that realigns your energy. Our thoughts and emotions deeply influence our energy, and when your chakras are balanced, maintaining a positive outlook and sense of well-being becomes easier. This transformative tool will support you as you embrace a new mindset and unlock your inner power.

Ultimately, what we all seek is happiness—and the truth is, it is already within us. The challenge, however, is that we often search for it outside of ourselves. But how can we truly receive happiness if we don't first feel it within?

Rewrite your story

To reiterate, your life is a reflection of your thoughts and actions. If you allow others to control your narrative, it is not their fault if things turn out poorly. You can't blame them because you gave them that power. Here is a simple truth—you will never attract abundance—whether it is material wealth, love or joy—if you keep blaming others and seeing yourself as a victim.

Your life is your choice. You need to know what you want and start moving in that direction. Even the smallest step can make a significant difference. Reading this book is one of those steps.

It is here to guide you in letting go, accepting your reality, embracing gratitude in the present and manifesting a bright, fulfilling future through mental detox and chakra healing.

I invite you to commit to this 21-day transformative journey. Imagine the person you can become, the life you can create and the happiness you can embrace.

It is time to rewrite your story, one day at a time. Dare to believe in the incredible person you are. Dare to live the life you deserve.

Reflection prompt

Take a moment to reflect on a past regret. What can you learn from it that will give you the confidence you need to go forward?

....

....

....

....

....

....

....

....

....

Remember, it is never too late. You have the power to change your life.

3 ••|•• Unveil Your Mind

"The true definition of mental illness is when the majority of your time is spent in the past or future, but rarely living in the realism of now."
—Shannon L. Alder

Have you ever thought about how much time you really have left in this world? According to the United Nations, the global life expectancy as of 2023 was 70.8 years for males and 76.0 years for females, with an overall average of 73.4 years. We are given about 27,000 days in a lifetime—on paper, it looks vast. Yet pause, and you see how quickly they vanish. Over 4,000 days slip away in working and commuting. More than a decade is spent in education—whether in school, college or vocational training—learning, growing and trying to find our way. Nearly one-third of life is lost to sleep. Then comes the everyday gauntlet: eating, cleaning, scrolling through social media, caring for loved ones and juggling endless responsibilities. And after all that—what remains? Perhaps only 2,000 days—or around six years—that are truly our own. Broken down, this means that every 12 years we get about one year for ourselves, or roughly one month each year to focus entirely on nurturing our soul, mind, heart and body.

That is why this 21-day journey is worth taking once a year—to reconnect with yourself mentally, emotionally and spiritually, and to care for the parts of you that are often overlooked. Just imagine: a handful of precious years reserved only for your healing, your purpose, your joy. Don't those days deserve your heart's full presence?

When we are so caught up in work, bills and the daily grind, we often forget that our mental health plays a huge role in how we spend our precious time. Did you know that nearly 1 in 8 people globally—nearly one billion—are struggling with their mental health (World Health Organization, 2022)? These are not just numbers. They are real people—people like you, me, our friends and our families.

Mental health matters. It affects how we feel, how we think and how we connect with the world. And if we don't take care of it, it can quietly steal away our happiness, bit by bit.

I have been there. I have had moments when everything felt overwhelming, when the joy I once had seemed to fade, and I found myself asking, *Why is this happening to me?* But through that experience, I learned something important—we often get so attached to who we think we are that we resist change even when it is exactly what we need. We cling to old habits, patterns and beliefs, as if they define us. Have you ever noticed how often you say things like, "This is just how I am," or, "I've always been this way"? But maybe, just maybe, it is time to rethink that.

Your happiness and well-being start with recognizing that you have the power to create a life that truly nourishes you. Together, we can make the most of those 2,000 days. Let us explore how to reclaim your time, your peace and your joy.

Release what is holding you back

But to do that, you need to let go of the beliefs and habits that no longer serve you. It is easy to stay stuck in the past, hoping things will change without actually changing anything about ourselves. But here is the truth—you can't expect improved results if you are still holding on to old patterns. If you keep being the same person, you will keep getting the same outcomes. It is that simple.

I know change isn't easy. It can be challenging, and it takes effort. But it all starts with understanding yourself—asking the right questions: *Am I where I want to be? Do I feel supported? Am I on the right path?* This journey begins with self-awareness—a moment to pause and check in with yourself, *How am I really doing right now?*

Know yourself

> "Knowing others is intelligence; knowing yourself is true wisdom. Mastering others is strength; mastering yourself is true power."—Laozi

Let us use a simple questionnaire. This isn't a test; it is just a way for you to uncover both the challenges you face and the good things you are already doing to take care of yourself. Don't worry: there are no "right" or "wrong" answers. Just be honest with yourself. Take a moment to really think about how you feel. For each question, choose any one option: never, rarely, sometimes, often, or always. By the end, you will have a clearer idea of where you stand mentally and emotionally.

Challenges

Do I often

- feel overwhelmed by stress?
- have trouble sleeping?
- experience changes in appetite?
- find it hard to focus or concentrate on tasks?
- feel fatigued or tired, even after resting?
- feel like avoiding social situations or isolating myself?
- experience feelings of sadness or hopelessness?
- feel anxious or worried about the future?
- have physical symptoms of stress, such as headaches or muscle tension?

Strengths

Do I often

- engage in physical activity that energizes me?
- engage in hobbies or activities that bring me joy?
- use healthy coping strategies, like deep breathing and journaling?
- talk about my feelings or seek support when I am struggling?
- Practise gratitude or acknowledge things I am thankful for?
- feel proud of my achievements, no matter how small?
- set goals for myself and work towards achieving them?
- take time for self-care, such as relaxation or pampering?
- try new things or step outside my comfort zone?

Interpreting the results

If you mostly answered *often* or *always* in the challenges section, it might be helpful to explore those feelings further. Stress, sleep issues or trouble focusing can really impact your daily life. You might consider reaching out to a mental health professional—they can help you cope better.

On the other hand, if you answered *often* or *always* in the strengths section, that shows you are actively doing things that support your mental well-being. Keep up those good habits because they can really make a difference in your overall health and happiness.

As you reflect on your answers, you might notice some patterns. Many people find stress and sleep challenging due to daily pressures, while others are better at seeking support or staying active. Recognizing these patterns can offer valuable insights into your habits and well-being.

> "Until you make the unconscious conscious, it will direct your life and you will call it fate."—C.G. Jung

Remember, recognizing your challenges is just as important as celebrating your strengths. Both are part of your journey of self-discovery and growth.

Love starts with you

> "Loving yourself isn't vanity; it's sanity."—Katrina Mayer

If the universe handed you someone to care for, wouldn't you treat them with love and kindness? Of course, you would. Yet, in our busy lives, we often forget to care for the most important person—ourselves. You are that person the universe entrusted to you. Just as you nurture others, you need love, attention and care too. It is not selfish; it is essential. It is time for a reset—a reboot. After all, no one is you, and that is your superpower.

Every morning, pause and ask yourself, "What can I do today to show myself love and care?" Let this simple question guide your actions. This small habit has the potential to transform your life in ways you never thought possible.

How to reboot yourself

I have put together a list of self-care practices that helped me on my journey, and I believe they can guide you towards a renewed sense of well-being. These habits are powerful tools that can shape the quality of our lives, leading to transformative changes. By incorporating them into your daily routine, you will begin to reboot your system—physically, emotionally and mentally.

Embrace the outdoors

"Fitness is like a relationship. You can't cheat and expect it
to work."—Unknown

Start by spending 20 to 30 minutes walking outside in the sunlight, breathing in fresh air. The sun boosts vitamin D, which is essential for your health and mood. Walking helps boost your mood because it increases blood flow and blood circulation to the brain and body. It will leave you feeling happier, less stressed and more energized.

Walking is not just good for your mental health—it is also beneficial for your gut health. Regular walking promotes healthy digestion, and when your gut is happy, your mind feels lighter too. Everything is connected. Studies have shown that a healthy gut supports mental well-being, so when you take care of your body, you are also nurturing your mind. Most people associate serotonin with the brain. After all, it is the "feel-good" neurotransmitter that regulates mood, sleep and appetite. What is less known is that nearly 90 per cent of the body's serotonin is produced in the gut.

Any kind of exercise—whether it is walking, running, yoga or even cycling—gets your body moving and your brain working. When you exercise, your brain releases endorphins, the "feel-good" hormones, while lowering cortisol, the stress hormone. Endorphins are the body's natural pain relievers and mood boosters. When you feel good, it becomes easier to make healthier choices, like eating better and doing more of what brings you joy. Isn't it amazing how everything is connected?

"All progress takes place outside the comfort zone."
—Michael John Bobak

Don't think of exercise as a chore. It is not something you have to do. Instead, look at it as a way to feel better and enjoy life more. Find an outdoor activity that makes you happy, get outside and soak up the sun and breathe in the fresh air. And feel the difference!

Practise affirmations

"I am not what has happened to me. I am what I choose to become."—Carl Jung

Words, just like thoughts and actions, have incredible power. They too have the ability to shape your reality. Every time you say something, you create an affirmation that impacts your life. In the vast landscape of personal development and self-discovery, a simple yet profound phrase stands out as a beacon of empowerment—I am." When you say "I am", you tap into your deepest and highest self. Your subconscious interprets it as a command, reinforcing your inner strength.

Be mindful of the words you choose because they hold the key to shaping our reality. Every time you say, "I am capable", "I deserve happiness", "I am worthy of love", you are not just describing yourself—you are defining your future. They can either build the life you desire or limit your potential. These words are not just a prelude to self-expression—they are a declaration of your identity and intent.

Affirmations can either hold you back or help you grow. Choose the ones that align with your goals and speak them with confidence. Make affirmations a part of your daily routine. Imagine beginning each day with positive affirmations that direct your actions towards your desired goals.

Try doing this first thing in the morning when your mind is clear. Stand in front of a mirror, look into your own eyes and speak your affirmations with conviction. For example, say, "I am enough" or "I am healing." This small act can transform how you approach each day and create a ripple effect of positive outcomes. You are worthy of every positive change you are inviting into your life.

Let go of what is holding you back

"Letting go means to come to the realization that some people are a part of your history, but not a part of your destiny."—Steve Maraboli

You cannot imagine the happiness you will feel when you begin letting go. It is like clearing out the clutter in your mind and heart, making room for more joy, love and peace.

Letting go isn't only about the people who hurt you—it is also about releasing the regrets that keep you tied to the past. Holding on to pain or missed chances only weighs you down. Not forgiving, whether others or yourself, is a way of punishing your own heart. It clouds your spirit, blocks healing and hinders growth.

I know from experience that learning to forgive and release regrets is essential because holding on to the past can stop you from enjoying the present and your future. Letting go isn't always easy, but once you do, you create space for peace and happiness to flow into your life.

A simple daily practice can help you with this. Try repeating phrases like "I forgive them" or "I forgive myself". When you do this consistently, you remind yourself to let go, bringing emotional relief. You truly deserve that peace.

Be grateful

"Joy is the simplest form of gratitude."—Karl Bath

Gratitude brings abundance. The more grateful you are, the more abundance you will invite into your life—not only in material things but in love, joy and meaningful experiences. When you take time to be thankful, the universe responds by sending even more blessings your way. Taking a moment to appreciate even the smallest experience shifts your mindset from scarcity to abundance. By doing this, we create a positive cycle that keeps growing. Remember, what you give is what you get.

To help build this habit, try journaling. Every day, write down five things you are grateful for. This practice shifts your mindset and helps you focus on what you have rather than what you lack. It is a simple but powerful way to invite more joy into your day. Embracing gratitude helps create a beautiful flow of positivity. Let gratitude be the foundation of your journey to joy—you absolutely deserve every wonderful thing that comes your way.

Find your inner calm

> "The quieter you become, the more you are able
> to hear."—Rumi

I recommend taking a pause every day to give your busy mind a break. People often make meditation seem mysterious, but it is actually quite simple. You might think it means completely silencing your thoughts, but that is a common misunderstanding. We can't stop our thoughts; it is part of being human. But what we can do is slow them down and learn to observe them without judgement, which comes with practice. Trust me, it is incredibly rewarding.

The beauty of this practice is that you can choose what works best for you. For some, chanting "Om" feels right. Others find peace in mindful breathing, while some discover a meditative state through jogging, walking or listening to music. There is no right or wrong way—what matters is finding what resonates with you and brings you a sense of calm and clarity.

> "Your calm mind is the ultimate weapon against your challenges. So relax."—Bryant McGill

As a beginner, all you need to do is focus on calming your mind and relaxing your body. Pay attention to your breathing, and if any thoughts pop up, gently guide your focus back to your breath. Start small—maybe just five minutes a day. As you get more comfortable, you can gradually spend more time in this peaceful state. This simple practice will help calm you and reconnect you with your truest self. You have got this, and you deserve this moment of peace.

Visualize your dreams

> "Visualization is daydreaming with a purpose."—Bo Bennett

You might have heard about visualization—it is a powerful technique. Many of my clients ask me about it. Let me share something important—visualization and affirmation go hand in hand. When you visualize, you make your affirmations stronger. But remember, visualization works based on who you are, not just what you want. *You attract what you are, not just what you wish for.*

For example, if you want to be a millionaire but think with a scarcity mindset, it will not work. You need to truly feel and live that abundance in your mind because your mind believes what you think. You have got to become that future version of yourself.

Here is how you can start: Every day, find a quiet spot, close your eyes and let go of distractions. Focus on your breath—inhaling for six counts, holding for three and exhaling for six. This rhythm will help calm your mind. Now, visualize your desired outcome—whether it is feeling more confident, joining a gym, finding a loving partner or landing your dream job. Allow yourself to truly feel what it is like to achieve that outcome.

But don't forget, visualization is just the first step. You need to be patient and take action(s) too. Visualizing your goals helps you align with them, but it is the actions you take each day that turn those dreams into reality. So, dream big—after all, dreams are free! Feel it, believe you have it and then take the steps to make it happen.

"I begin by imagining the impossible and end by accomplishing the impossible."—Sri Chinmoy

You have the incredible power to rewire your own brain—no neuroscientist, lightning bolts or meditation caves are required. Yes, you read that right. With 86 billion neurons, or brain cells, that constantly send signals and form pathways, you can rewire these connections through practices like visualization and meditation. These practices can gently shift your brainwaves and open the door to more joy, peace and resilience in your life. Just remember, while visualization and meditation are powerful tools, they work best when paired with action. Embrace these practices and start taking those small, meaningful steps together.

Share your feelings

"Courage starts with showing up and letting ourselves be seen."—Brené Brown

Trust me, there is incredible strength in vulnerability. I know how isolating anxiety and stress can feel, and when you are feeling low, reaching out can seem difficult. But negative thoughts have a way of sticking around, sometimes making it hard to take that first step towards connection. But the relief and support you gain from sharing are genuinely worth it.

When you open up to someone, doesn't it feel like a weight has lifted off your shoulders? Talking with a friend, family member, or partner who listens without judgement can be incredibly freeing. These simple moments of connection do more than just ease stress; they deepen the bonds you share with others and remind you that you don't have to face everything alone.

When you express what you are going through, you invite support and understanding. This can shift how you view both yourself and your challenges, giving your mental health a meaningful boost. Remember, you are not alone on this journey.

Take a moment now to check in with yourself.

- Are you prioritizing your well-being?

- Are you setting aside time for activities that bring you joy?

Just as you care for others, you deserve the same love and care. Your journey to a happier, healthier you starts with a simple choice—to put yourself first. *Commit to yourself.*

Who's in your corner?

Now, think about the people in your life who are always there for you. These are the people who make up your support network. Having people you can rely on makes a big difference when you are facing tough times.

Reflection prompt

Who are the three people I can reach out to when I am feeling stressed or need someone to talk to?

....

....

....

....

....

....

....

....

How can I strengthen those relationships even more?

....

....

....

....

....

....

....

....

....

....

4   Unlock the Secrets of Your Energy Flow

"Your energy introduces you before you even speak, and balancing your chakras will help you project your highest self."
—Gabrielle Bernstein

Have you ever felt like you are stuck in a rut, unsure why things aren't moving forward? Maybe you are constantly tired or overwhelmed for reasons you can't pinpoint. What if those feelings are your body's way of whispering that something deeper needs your attention?

I remember the day I first discovered chakras—it felt like finding a hidden map to the energy that had been guiding me all along. The concept wasn't mystical or distant; on the contrary, it felt familiar, like it had always been part of me, subtly shaping my thoughts, emotions and health.

This discovery changed everything for me. I realized that my well-being isn't just about my mind or body—it is about harmonizing all parts of myself, including my mind, body, heart and soul.

Around that time, I was preparing for a big career change, which was exciting but also brought up fears and doubts. Looking back, I realize my root chakra—the energy centre linked to security and stability—was probably blocked. I was trying to manifest my dream life while also working to create it, but part of me felt like I was standing on unsteady ground.

Recognizing this gave me a new perspective. Understanding the chakras became a powerful tool—one that encouraged me to confront these insecurities directly. It felt like tapping into a new source of clarity and confidence, a sense of inner steadiness that made moving forward feel less daunting and more aligned with my true self.

Understand your chakras

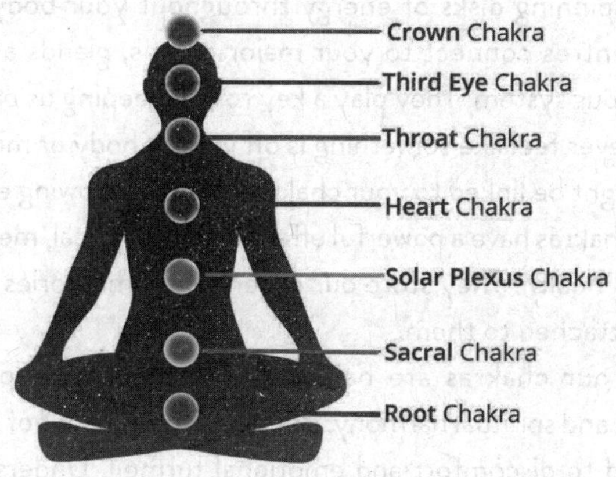

Source: Image generated by AI

Image 4.1: Your Seven Chakras

The seven chakras and their locations

1. Root chakra (*muladhara*): Base of the spine, tailbone area
2. Sacral chakra (*svadhisthana*): Lower belly just below the navel/pelvis region

3. Solar plexus chakra (*manipura*): Upper abdomen in the middle just below the ribcage

4. Heart chakra (*anahata*): Centre of the chest, at the heart level

5. Throat chakra (*vishuddha*): Throat area

6. Third eye chakra (*ajna*): Forehead, between the eyes

7. Crown chakra (*sahasrara*): Top of the head

In yoga philosophy, the word "chakra" means wheel. You can picture them as spinning disks of energy throughout your body. These energy centres connect to your major organs, glands and even your nervous system. They play a key role in keeping us balanced.

If you ever feel like something is off in your body or mind, that feeling might be linked to your chakras. There is growing evidence that our chakras have a powerful effect on our physical, mental and emotional health. They store our experiences, memories and the feelings attached to them.

When our chakras are balanced, we experience physical, emotional and spiritual harmony. But when they are out of balance, it can lead to discomfort and emotional turmoil. Understanding your chakras can help you discover what is holding you back and guide you on your journey to well-being.

How chakra imbalance affects you

When a chakra is blocked or out of alignment, it often shows up as physical discomfort or emotional tension. For instance, a blocked throat chakra might make it difficult to for you to express yourself honestly, while a blocked heart chakra can create feelings of isolation.

The more I explored chakras, the more I realized how they hold significant power over our well-being, and by tuning into these energy centres, we can start to receive subtle messages from within.

Recognizing when your energy feels stuck or out of sync is a cue to look deeper. When you pay attention to these signals, you can make small changes that help restore balance. So, why not begin listening to what your body, mind and soul are trying to tell you?

Recognize the signs of your blocked chakras

You might wonder, *How can I start to recognize and work with these energy centres to feel better and more in tune with myself?* A good place to start is understanding each chakra—what it represents and how it affects you physically, emotionally and mentally. By connecting with each one, you will have a roadmap to help you make small, meaningful adjustments in your life.

I will walk you through each of the seven chakras, from the base of your spine up to the crown of your head, helping you connect with the deeper energy and wisdom within you. Take your time as you read, and remember: this is about discovering your unique path to well-being. As we explore the ancient practice of chakra healing, we will dive deeper into the significance of these energy centres and how we can best nurture them to promote lasting health and vitality. Let us start at the foundation—your sense of safety and stability.

	Physical Symptoms	Emotional Symptoms
Root Chakra Muladhara	Fatigue, Constipation, Lower Back/Leg Issues	Fear, Insecurity, Anxiety
Sacral Chakra Svadhisthana	Fatigue, Constipation, Lower Back/Leg Issues	Creative Block, Intimacy issues, Suppressed Emotions
Solar Plexus Chakra Manipura	Ulcers, Digestive Issues, Liver/Pancreas Disorders	Anger, Low Self-Esteem, Lack of Willpower
Heart Chakra Anahata	Asthma, Upper Back Pain, Heart/Lung Issues	Jealousy, Lack of Empathy, Inability to Forgive
Throat Chakra Vishuddha	Sore Throat, Thyroid Issues, Neck/Shoulder Tension	Dishonesty, Fear of Speaking, Difficulty Expressing
Third Eye Chakra Ajna	Headaches, Vision Problems, Sleep Disturbances	Confusion, Overthinking, Poor Intuition
Crown Chakra Sahasrara	Migraines, Mental Disorders, Neurological Issues	Spiritual crisis, Disconnection, Lack of Purpose

Source: Image generated by AI

Image 4.2: Blocked Chakras and Their Symptoms

Root chakra (muladhara)

The root chakra, or muladhara, is located at the base of your spine. Picture it as a sturdy red ball right at your tailbone. This chakra is all about feeling secure and grounded, like the roots of a tree that keep it stable.

When this energy centre is blocked, you might feel various issues. Physically, you could experience lower back pain, sciatica or problems with your legs and feet. Emotionally, you might struggle with feelings of insecurity, fear of change or a lack of trust. Mentally, it could be hard to concentrate and you might feel disconnected from reality or notice anxiety creeping in. You might also find it tough to make decisions about your basic needs.

Sacral chakra (svadhisthana)

Moving up, we reach the sacral chakra, or *svadhisthana*. This chakra is located in your lower belly, just a couple of inches below your navel. Picture it as a vibrant orange orb that represents the feelings of creativity and emotional balance.

When this chakra is out of balance, you might face several issues. Physically, you could have lower back pain, reproductive problems or irregular menstrual cycles. Emotionally, you might feel weighed down by guilt, experience mood swings or struggle with intimacy and self-worth. Mentally, it may be hard for you to express your creativity. You might feel blocked in your ideas or find it difficult to enjoy life's pleasures.

Solar plexus chakra (manipura)

The solar plexus chakra, or manipura, is located in the upper belly, between your belly button and the bottom of your chest, a couple of fingers above your belly button. I want you to picture it as a bright yellow sun, shining with your personal power and confidence.

When this chakra is blocked, you might feel unmotivated and unsure of yourself—like a balloon that has lost its air, deflated and lacking the drive to soar. Physically, you could experience digestive issues, like bloating or stomach cramps, and you might feel low energy or fatigue. Emotionally, you may struggle with feelings of anger, frustration or worthlessness. Mentally, it could be tough for you to make decisions or take charge of your life, set boundaries or stay focused on your goals. You might also notice self-doubt creeping in.

Heart chakra (anahata)

The heart chakra, or anahata, sits in the centre of your chest, symbolizing love and compassion, glowing a beautiful green colour.

When this chakra is out of balance, you might notice some physical issues like heart problems, chest pain or even respiratory problems. Emotionally, you could find it hard to forgive or love and feel jealous and lonely. You might struggle with connecting to others, and it is a tough place to be, especially when we all crave love and understanding. Mentally, you may have trouble focusing on positive thoughts or feel stuck in negative patterns and making it hard to let go and forgive.

Throat chakra (vishuddha)

The throat chakra, or vishuddha is all about communication and self-expression, and it is located right at your throat. Picture it as a stunning blue gem.

When it is blocked, physically, you might experience issues like a sore throat, neck pain or even thyroid problems. Emotionally, it can feel really tough to share your thoughts and feelings. You might hold back, finding it hard to say what you truly feel or believe. And that can be frustrating. Mentally, you may struggle with self-doubt and feel anxious about expressing your thoughts, opinions and creativity.

Third eye chakra (ajna)

The third eye chakra, or ajna, is located right between your eyebrows and looks like a deep indigo jewel. It is connected to your intuition and insight.

When this chakra is blocked, you might notice some physical issues, like headaches, eye strain or sinus problems. Emotionally, negative thoughts may swirl in your mind, making it tough to feel balanced. You might feel disconnected from your inner wisdom or struggle to trust your intuition. It is like having a foggy windshield— you can't see clearly ahead and that can feel overwhelming. Mentally, you may find it difficult to focus, make decisions or feel stuck in your thoughts.

Crown chakra (sahasrara)

The crown chakra, or sahasrara, sits right at the top of your head, shining like a bright white light. This chakra connects us to spirituality and our sense of purpose.

When this chakra is blocked, you might notice some physical issues, like headaches or trouble sleeping. You could also feel really tired, making it hard to find the energy to engage with life. Emotionally, you might feel lost, disconnected or even apathetic. You may struggle with feelings of isolation or a lack of meaning or purpose in your life. Mentally, you may find it hard to focus or accept new ideas and you might feel confused about your direction in life. It is like standing on a high cliff, wanting to leap into the unknown but feeling afraid of what lies beneath.

Each of these seven chakras plays a big role in your life, whether you realize it or not. They influence how you think, how you feel, and how you connect with yourself and others. When you understand them, you can navigate life's ups and downs with more awareness and balance.

So, how are your chakras feeling right now? Take a moment to check in with yourself.

Know your energy flow

Understanding your chakras can help you feel more balanced and in tune with yourself. When one or more of your chakras are out of balance, you might feel stuck, uncertain or disconnected. This simple questionnaire will guide you in reflecting on your chakras and gaining insights into where you might need more attention.

As you go through each question, think about how it relates to your life. Pay attention to where you feel strong and confident, and where things feel off. This awareness is the first step towards healing and creating more harmony in your life.

For each question, score yourself from 1 to 5:

1 means never,

2 means rarely,

3 means sometimes,

4 means often, and

5 means always.

At the end, take a moment to reflect on your total score for each chakra. It will help you understand where you are thriving and where you might need more balance. Your total score for each chakra will range from 3 to 15.

Root chakra (Score: ___ out of 15)

I often ...

- Feel pain in my legs or lower back, or struggle with constipation.

- Feel anxious or find it hard to focus or concentrate.

- Worry about my financial security or stability in life.

Sacral chakra (Score: ___ out of 15)

I often ...

- have pelvic pain or experience menstrual or urinary issues.

- feel blocked creatively or have trouble coming up with new ideas.

- experience mood swings or feel distant from others emotionally.

Solar plexus chakra (Score: ___ out of 15)

I often ...

- suffer from digestive issues or feel tired or low energy often.

- feel uncertain about my decisions or doubt my ability to achieve my goals.

- feel powerless, as if I can't take control of my own life.

Heart chakra (Score: ___ out of 15)

I often ...

- feel a tightness or discomfort or pain in my chest.

- find it hard to express love or empathy to others.

- hold on to grudge or find it difficult to forgive myself or others.

Throat chakra (Score: ___ out of 15)

I often ...

- have throat discomfort like soreness or tightness or deal with frequent coughing.

- feel confused or stuck when making decisions or stuck in my thoughts.

- struggle to express my true feelings with others.

Third eye chakra (Score: ___ out of 15)

I often …

- get headaches or feel strain in my eyes.

- feel unclear or uncertain about the direction of my life.

- find it difficult to trust my intuition or feel disconnected from my inner wisdom.

Crown chakra (Score: ___ out of 15)

I often …

- suffer from headaches or have trouble sleeping.

- feel disconnected from my sense of purpose or unsure of my goals.

- feel isolated or cut off from a larger community or spiritual connection.

Reflect on your scores for each chakra

Now that you have assessed your chakras, take a moment to reflect on the areas where your scores are higher. These may indicate potential imbalances that could benefit from more attention and nurturing.

12–15: You may be experiencing significant imbalance and disconnection in this area. Feelings of insecurity or emotional blockages may be prominent. Consider seeking professional help to address these issues and explore practices to nurture this chakra.

10–12: You might have some balance in this chakra, but there are areas that could benefit from further attention. Focus on enhancing this chakra through activities that foster growth.

7–9: You generally feel balanced and connected in this area, but there may still be room for growth. Continue nurturing your energy through self-care practices and reflection.

3–6: You feel fully connected and aligned with this chakra, experiencing harmony and strength. Consider sharing your insights and practices with others to inspire them on their journey towards balance.

This questionnaire is a starting point for exploring your chakra awareness. Reflecting on your scores will guide you on your journey towards balance and harmony.

A simple practice to tune into your chakras

To start connecting with your chakras, take a few minutes each day to sit quietly and breathe deeply. Close your eyes and picture each chakra as a spinning disc of energy, moving smoothly from the base of your spine up to the top of your head. Notice any areas that feel tense or blocked, and imagine the energy there loosening and flowing freely.

This practice doesn't need to be long—just a few minutes each day can make a difference. Over time, you will likely find yourself feeling more balanced and aware of your own energy. Listening to these subtle messages is the first step towards harmonizing all parts of yourself.

Isn't it time we all started listening to what our bodies, minds and souls are trying to tell us?

How to reclaim your energy

When the chakras open, life force flows freely and healing begins from within. If any of your chakras are blocked or out of balance, you can take simple steps to help yourself heal.

For your root chakra, grounding exercises can really make a difference. You might find it helpful to walk barefoot on grass, practise mindfulness or do deep breathing. Mindfulness means being fully present in the moment without judgement. It is about gently observing your thoughts, emotions and body sensations as they come and go, with curiosity and acceptance. This practice helps you feel calmer, more stable and connected to yourself. These small activities can help you feel more secure and rooted. You could also try grounding yoga poses to connect deeply with the earth.

When it comes to your sacral chakra, try to nurture it by engaging in creative activities like painting, dancing or writing. You can also explore emotional release techniques, like journaling or talking to someone you trust. This will help you reconnect with your feelings and enjoy life's pleasures again. Engaging in water-based activities, like swimming or even a mindful bath, can help soothe and balance this chakra.

If you are working on your solar plexus chakra, positive affirmations can really boost your confidence. Setting small, achievable goals will help you build your personal power. Try core-strengthening exercises to feel energized and strong from within. Practising breath work, like diaphragmatic breathing, can also ignite energy and power in this area.

For your heart chakra, self-love is essential. Daily affirmations can be a great practice, and don't forget to practise forgiveness—both for yourself and others. Spend time with loved ones or do something that brings out compassion in you. This will help open your heart to love. Another great practice is heart-opening yoga poses to release any tension and open yourself to giving and receiving love.

When you are focusing on your throat chakra, practise speaking openly and honestly. Journaling, speaking in front of a mirror, or having honest conversations with people you care about can help you express yourself more easily. Singing or chanting can also help clear this chakra and improve your ability to communicate your truth.

To nurture your third eye chakra, mindfulness and meditation can help you tune into your intuition. Try visualization exercises to strengthen your insight and see things more clearly. You could also explore dream journaling to enhance your intuition and connect with your subconscious. Dream journaling is the practice of writing down your dreams as soon as you wake up. Some dream journalers sketch what they see and some even record their dreams. Over time, this helps you notice patterns, symbols and messages from your subconscious, which will enhance self-awareness, creativity and emotional processing.

Finally, for your crown chakra, spiritual practices, like meditation or prayer, can help you feel more connected to the universe. Take time to reflect on your life's purpose and find communities that support your spiritual journey. Another great way to nurture this chakra is spending time in nature, gazing at the sky or stargazing to remind yourself of your connection to the universe.

By recognizing these signs and nurturing your chakras, you can unlock your full potential and live a more balanced life. Remember, your healing journey begins with you.

Embrace your healing journey

There is incredible power in understanding your chakras. When you tune into your energy and emotions, you can uncover the root causes of what is bothering you. It is not about pushing away your feelings; it is about listening to your body and finding ways to heal from within yourself.

As I worked on my chakras, I began to notice positive changes in my life; for example, I felt more connected to my purpose. It was not about trying to be perfect or "fixing" myself; it was about learning to flow with my own energy. Chakra healing isn't something you do once and forget—it is an ongoing journey of tuning in, letting go, and realigning yourself.

Your energy is always evolving, and the more you stay in tune with it, the more empowered you will feel to face whatever life throws at you. When you approach life with this mindset, you begin to feel more grounded, peaceful and connected to both yourself and the world around you. It is like a gentle awakening, where you realize how deeply your thoughts, emotions and physical health are linked.

"Your self-love is a medicine for the earth."—Yung Pueblo

Healing is about giving yourself the space to grow and understanding that this journey is uniquely yours. As you explore your chakras, be patient with yourself. It is okay if insights don't come right away or if things don't change overnight. Trust that they will unfold in their own time, in a way that feels natural and right for you. Be open to the possibility of healing, growth and discovering the amazing person you truly are.

Now, take a moment to close your eyes, breathe deeply and gently focus on each chakra from root to crown, noticing any sensations, warmth, tingling or areas of tension:

Which chakra felt the most alive or active for you, and why?

....

....

....

....

....

....

....

....

....

What did you learn about yourself through this process?

....

....

....

....

....

… …

… …

… …

… …

Which chakra surprised you the most, and why?

… …

… …

… …

… …

… …

… …

… …

… …

… …

5   Ultimate Reboot—The Journey Begins

"The only person you are destined to become is the person you decide to be."—Ralph Waldo Emerson

Every change is a chance to redefine who you are. Are you ready to embark on this powerful 21-day journey of healing, aligning and renewing your mind, body and soul?

I am inviting you to fully commit to this experience. Because in every change lies the seed of a new beginning. It is going to be a time of incredible growth and self-discovery. Each day will be an opportunity to grow, heal, and connect more deeply with yourself and the world around you. Together, we will build awareness and intention, strengthening your mind, body and spirit. Embrace this journey with an open heart, knowing that each step brings you closer to the vibrant, empowered person you are meant to be. Change isn't just possible—it is your right. Because if you don't change, you don't grow. If you don't grow, you aren't really living.

Let me walk you through how this journey will unfold. It is broken down into three weeks, each with its own focus. I will provide tools and exercises to help with personal growth and healing. My goal is to help you unlock your full potential. Are you excited?

"Believe you can and you're halfway there."—Theodore Roosevelt

Week 1: Forgiveness—let go of the past

"In the process of letting go you will lose many things from the past, but you will find yourself."—Deepak Chopra

In this first week, you will explore the power of forgiveness. Think about it—holding on to past pain and regrets only keeps you stuck. Those old wounds can prevent you from moving forward and living the life you want. Alongside forgiveness, you will be working with your chakras each day to release blocked energy and promote healing in specific areas.

Forgiveness is a gift you give *yourself*—it is your superpower to let go of the past and create space for new possibilities. The past is a teacher, not a prison. It is time to break free and embrace the amazing future that is waiting for you.

Week 2: Gratitude—embrace the present

"Gratitude makes sense of our past, brings peace for today and creates a vision for tomorrow."—Melody Beattie

In Week 2, you will focus on gratitude and being present. Take a moment right now to appreciate the beauty around you and recognize the small joys in your life. Gratitude isn't just a positive feeling; it is a powerful tool for shifting your perspective and opening your heart to all that life has to offer.

This week, you will also work on clearing and balancing a different chakra each day. This combination will help you anchor your awareness in the present moment, allowing positive energy to flow more freely. Each moment of appreciation is a step towards a more fulfilling life. By embracing the present, you create a mindset that attracts abundance and joy into your world. It is truly magical.

Week 3: Manifestation—shape your future

"The clearer you are, the faster you manifest."—Dr Joe Vitale

Finally, in Week 3, you will set your intentions and focus on manifesting the bright, successful and joyful future you deserve. Manifestation is not just about wishing for something—it is about aligning your mind, body and energy with your goals.

This week, we will clear any remaining energy blockages that could hold you back by working with a different chakra each day. Balanced and healed chakras amplify your manifesting power, allowing your intentions to flow with greater clarity and ease. To move forward, we need to let go of the past and embrace the present. That is how we build the future we want.

Every affirmation and intention you set this week will be a building block for the life you envision. Believe in your power to create positive change, and watch your dreams come to life. It is all within your reach.

How to use this book

The Ultimate Reboot is your chance to heal, grow and change— one small step at a time. Healing doesn't happen overnight; it is a gradual and beautiful process. Every single step, no matter how small, is a move towards a healthier mind, body and soul.

Remember, your wound is not your fault, but your healing is your responsibility.

Each day, you will engage in a simple practice designed to support your healing. It is not about perfection—it is about progress. These exercises are here to help you reconnect with yourself and find your own path to growth. You might not notice big changes at first, *but trust the journey*. With each step, you are investing in yourself, and that is what truly matters.

Your daily rituals

Set a morning reminder

Begin your day by writing down a short paragraph in the worksheet. It gently centres your mind, reminding you of the day's focus and aligning your energy with your intention.

Recite the affirmation for the day

When you wake up, stand in front of the mirror and look into your eyes. Say your affirmation out loud with confidence. Repeat it throughout the day whenever you can. Let these words stay with you, helping you feel strong and centred.

Two daily exercises—balanced support for healing

Each day, you will engage in two simple exercises that take just a few minutes each. Together, they support your healing journey by helping you care for your mind, body and soul. You don't need to do them one after the other—you can space them out throughout the day. For example, you might choose to do one in the morning and the other in the evening, or at any time that feels right for you.

Exercise 1—chakra-focused action

For the next seven days, choose one person, situation, event, goal, dream or aspect of your life to focus on. Each day, take one small, intentional step that helps you move towards healing and balance in your energy centres (chakras). These action steps are designed to gently open, align and restore the flow of energy throughout your body and life. Progress is more important than perfection—allow yourself the space to grow and heal one step at a time.

Exercise 2—mental health reflection

Each day, spend a few minutes exploring your thoughts, feelings and experiences. Choose a person, situation, goal or event to reflect on through journaling or quiet contemplation. This exercise helps you build awareness, gain clarity and support your emotional well-being. Some prompts may also touch upon chakra-related themes, offering deeper insight into how your energy and mindset are connected.

HOW THESE WORK TOGETHER

Though each exercise has a slightly different focus—one more on chakra healing and action, and the other more on mental health and reflection—they are deeply connected. Together, they help you build resilience, clarity, and balance in both your mind and energy.

Healing is a journey, not a destination. These exercises are tools you can turn to whenever you need support—guiding you towards greater awareness, inner peace and a deeper connection with yourself.

Meditate or chant the beej mantra

Set aside 10–15 minutes each day to meditate. Let it be your time to relax, breathe and reconnect with the present moment.

Source: Image generated by AI

Image 5.1: Beej Mantras for the Seven Chakras

Chanting beej mantras can gently support the healing of your body, mind, body and soul. Research shows that repeating these sounds enhances brain waves associated with focus, relaxation and emotional balance. It can reduce stress and anxiety, sharpen memory, and bring a deep sense of calm and centredness. Even subtle physiological effects—like synchronized heart–brain rhythms and deeper relaxation—have been observed during chanting. When you chant with awareness, you are not just repeating sounds; you are tuning your mind, body and energy, allowing your chakras to flow more freely.

Practise yoga

Practise yoga in the morning, on an empty stomach if possible, or during your regular exercise routine. Do it with the intention of healing. Since yoga is both a physical and spiritual practice, the asanas are not only exercises for your body but also your mind, emotions and spirit, making it the perfect practice for balancing your chakras.

Eat the food for the day

Eat with purpose. Focus on feeding your mind, body and soul with foods that support your healing. As you eat, think about the intention for the day and let the food nourish you in both body and spirit.

Wrap up the day with a closing ritual

Before you go to sleep, take a few minutes to think about your day. What did you learn? What mistakes did you make? This reflection helps you grow. Be honest with yourself—what can you do better next time? Reflecting like this helps you move forward with more wisdom. Understand yourself and continue growing.

Say a promise to yourself

Your commitment means everything. Your life is in your hands, and you have the power to shape it. This journey isn't about quick fixes—it is about real, lasting change. I understand if you have doubts; that is completely normal. Change can be slow, but it is happening. Every small step you take matters.

This isn't just about ticking off tasks—it is about making a promise to yourself. It is about discovering who you are, finding peace within and building deeper connections with those around you. You have the strength to create the life you want.

By the end of this journey, you will feel more connected to yourself, with the tools to keep growing for the rest of your life. You are not alone in this process. Let us take this one step at a time, knowing that each effort, no matter how small, brings us closer to the life we deserve.

This is your time. Uncover your potential, make it real and create the life you have been dreaming of. You are worth it.

I believe in you.

> "We know what we are, but know not what we may be."—William Shakespeare

Engagement tips

As you progress through this journey, consider sharing your experiences with a community or an accountability partner. This connection will enhance your growth and keep you motivated.

WEEK 1

6   Forgiveness—Let Go of the Past

"Without forgiveness, there's no future."—Desmond Tutu

Welcome to Week 1 of our 21-day journey towards mental detox and chakra healing. This is your time for growth, reflection and transformation. Just remember that you are taking a significant step towards a healthier, happier you.

Holding on to the past can make you feel stuck and heavy. This can lead to mental health challenges, physical problems and difficulties in relationships. However, forgiveness is a powerful tool that helps heal those wounds. It breaks the chains of hurt and resentment, opening the door to fresh perspectives and allowing you to see life with compassion.

Forgiveness isn't a sign of weakness; it is a testament to your strength. It doesn't mean giving someone another chance to hurt you. Instead, it means releasing the grip that pain has on your heart. It is about learning from your experiences and recognizing that you deserve peace and happiness. Remember, as long as you are tied to your past, true happiness will remain out of reach. Forgiveness creates space for new opportunities in your life.

Each day, you will engage in activities that take about 45 minutes to an hour. Feel free to break them up throughout your day, making them a natural part of your routine. Commit to these practices, and watch how they reshape your thinking and transform your life. You can revisit these activities even after the 21 days. This book will be your personal diary and guide as you navigate life.

As you embark on this journey, embrace each moment. Acknowledge the courage it takes to confront your past, and honour your resilience as you move forward. Each step you take is a testament to your strength.

I wish you all the best on this journey. Remember, you are not just changing your mindset; you rewriting your story.

Day 1 : Forgiveness—discover the medicine within

> "The first step in forgiveness is the willingness to forgive."—Marianne Williamson

Have you ever felt a hurt so deep it just wouldn't go away? I have. We get stuck on those painful memories, replaying them over and over again in our minds like a broken record. Isn't it emotionally draining?

We know forgiveness is the answer, right? But actually doing it? That can feel impossible, like climbing the highest mountain. That struggle between wanting to let go and holding on to the pain? I get it. It is tough.

For me, forgiveness has been like finding my way back to inner peace. It is about acknowledging that hurt, that pain you have carried. When you forgive, you are breaking free from those chains of pain. You are taking that first, brave step towards a happier future.

And guess what? Forgiveness acts like a powerful medicine for your mind, body and soul. Studies show that practising forgiveness can lower your blood pressure, boost your immunity and even reduce chronic pain. It can help ease anxiety and depression too. When you release negative feelings, like anger and bitterness, you open the door to a happier, freer you. Don't you want to truly change how you feel, inside and out?

Find your ground

Your root chakra and forgiveness are deeply connected. When it is balanced, you feel safe, grounded and healthy. But when your root chakra is blocked by past hurts and resentment, it leaves you feeling unsteady and insecure. Forgiveness is one of the keys to unlocking that block. It helps you release that heavy weight of negativity you have been carrying.

It is time to let go of the past. You deserve to feel grounded, at peace and truly healed. You deserve to feel that sense of security and stability.

Worksheet 1: Forgiveness and the root chakra worksheet for restoring your foundation

Write down, "Today, I take my first step towards healing by releasing the anger that has held me back, letting go of the past. I am reclaiming my peace and strength, and planting a seed of forgiveness within myself. This is not for anyone else—it is for me. I deserve to feel light, whole and free, and I am ready to embrace lasting peace."

Affirmations for forgiveness to anchor your day

- "I forgive myself and feel safe in my body."
- "I release anger and ground myself in peace."
- "I am secure and let go of the past."

Exercise 1.1: Acknowledge the pain and ground yourself

This seven-day journey focuses on forgiving a specific person or incident that has deeply impacted you. Each day, you will explore a different aspect of forgiveness, gradually releasing pain and reclaiming peace.

Today, start by connecting with the earth to ground yourself. Stand barefoot outside and feel the earth beneath you. Breathe deeply, letting go of heaviness with each exhale. Imagine the earth absorbing your emotional weight, leaving you lighter and more at ease.

Acknowledge the pain—it has disrupted your stability and affected your root chakra, tied to your sense of security. Write down on a piece of paper what you are ready to release—anger, guilt or regret? And why?

Tear the paper and bury it, symbolizing a release of burdens. This practice isn't about forgetting—it is about freeing yourself from resentment and making space for healing. Each step in this process opens a path to understanding, empathy and inner growth.

Forgiveness and beej mantra meditation for the root chakra

"Lam" (pronounced lahm or lum) is the mantra for the root chakra. When you combine this mantra with grounding techniques explained earlier, you tap into a powerful tool for balancing your root chakra. This fosters the emotional security you need for forgiveness to emerge naturally. By healing your root chakra, you strengthen your ability to forgive and let go of emotional pain. The more grounded and secure you feel, the easier it becomes to release what has been holding you back. Remember, you have the power to heal and with each step you take, you move closer to a life filled with peace and freedom.

- Sit comfortably sit in a lotus position or in a chair, with your feet grounded and your palms resting on your knees.

- Close your eyes, breathe deeply and set the intention to forgive, visualizing the release of emotional pain.

- Visualize strong roots extending from your spine deep into the earth, connecting you to the earth's core.

- Inhale deeply, then exhale while chanting "Lam". Picture red energy expanding from your root chakra, helping you release your fear, insecurity and emotional pain. Continue to chant for 5–10 minutes, feeling that red energy grounding you and strengthening your connection to the earth.

- Now, think of the person or situation you want to forgive. Visualize them surrounded by a warm red light, dissolving your anger and pain. As you do this, affirm, "We all are learning, and we all make mistakes. I forgive you, and please forgive me." Repeat this a few times, and imagine that person gently vanishing into the air.

- Gently bring your focus back to your breath. Slowly open your eyes and express your gratitude to Mother Earth, saying, "Thank you for making me feel safe and secure, and for helping me release all emotional pain. I embrace this sense of peace and joy, allowing it to fill my mind, body and soul."

- Finally, take a moment to reflect on your experience. How do you feel now? Allow yourself some time for the meditation's effects to settle in.

Yoga for the root chakra: Forgiveness and emotional release

Start your day with some light yoga to release tension and stimulate the root chakra.

Asana 1.1: Warrior I (Virabhadrasana I)

This empowering posture encourages strength and resilience, helping to cultivate the inner courage needed to confront past hurts and move forward with forgiveness. The Warrior series (Warrior I, II and III) is a sequence of standing poses that build strength, focus and balance. Each pose has different physical and energetic qualities that can correspond to various chakras.

Asana 1.2: Child's Pose (Balasana)

Restorative pose fosters a sense of safety and comfort, allowing you to release tension and emotional blockages, creating space for forgiveness and healing.

Food for the root chakra

Foods like beetroots, sweet potatoes and red lentils together create a nourishing, grounding meal that promotes stability and emotional well-being, while providing the physical and emotional strength needed to support the process of forgiveness. These foods help balance energy and nourish the body, encouraging emotional healing. Incorporating them into your meals can help restore calm and clarity as you continue on your path to forgiveness. Remember to eat mindfully by focusing on each bite, thus allowing your body and mind to fully absorb the nourishment.

Exercise 1.2: Set your forgiveness intention

The forgiveness intention exercise begins with identifying three people or situations that still trigger feelings of hurt or anger. Take time to write down what happened and how these experiences have affected you emotionally and mentally. Be honest—explore the deeper reasons behind your pain. Then, set a clear intention for your forgiveness journey, focusing on finding peace and healing for yourself. Visualize the emotional burden being lifted from your body as you commit to releasing it. End with positive affirmations that reinforce your intention, like "I choose to let go" or "I am worthy of healing". This process aligns with your root chakra, grounding you in a journey towards freedom and emotional balance.

Who are three people or what are the three situations that still trigger feelings of hurt or anger for you?

1.

2.

3.

What emotions come up when you think about them?

……

……

……

……

……

……

……

……

……

How have these feelings impacted your mental well-being?

……

……

……

....

....

....

....

....

....

....

What is the one small step you can take right now to release these feelings and feel lighter?

....

....

....

....

....

....

....

....

....

Closing ritual: Reflect on forgiveness and healing

As you conclude Day 1, find a quiet space and sit comfortably.
Reflect on what you have experienced today.

*What emotions are you holding on to that are preventing you from
forgiving others?*

....

....

....

....

....

....

....

....

....

How can you release them to feel more stable and secure?

....

....

....

....

A promise to myself

Date:

Today, as I reflect on the steps I have taken towards forgiveness and healing. I feel...

I let go of the past; I am safe and secure.

Remember, forgiveness doesn't mean forgetting; it is about learning from the past and releasing its emotional grip, freeing yourself from hurt. It is a personal journey of healing, allowing you to move forward with peace. You deserve to feel secure and at ease.

Day 2 : Forgiveness—unpack hurt and find peace

"Forgiveness is the only way to heal."—Don Miguel Ruiz

When was the last time you truly forgave someone? It was tough, isn't it? But I want you to know that forgiveness is incredibly powerful because it has the ability to change your life, bringing you closer to happiness and healthier relationships.

Imagine you are carrying a heavy backpack filled with rocks. Each rock represents a hurt, betrayal or disappointment you have been holding on to. That weight makes life feel heavier, doesn't it? It drags you down. But what if you could start taking those rocks out, one by one?

Research suggests that forgiveness plays a crucial role in maintaining healthy and satisfying relationships. As you forgive, you begin to lighten your load. With each rock gone, you create space for joy, peace and stronger connections. Don't you want that lightness, that freedom and that peace in your life?

Release, heal and create

Forgiveness runs deep in your sacral chakra, shaping your emotions, creativity, sexual energy and the way you connect with others.

When it is balanced, you feel joy, harmony and a deep connection with others.

But when your sacral chakra is blocked by past hurt, guilt and resentment, it drains your energy, making it hard to feel joy and connection. It is painful to feel stuck like that, I know.

By letting go of the emotional weight you have been carrying, you create more space for love, creativity and connection. It allows you to move past the pain, rebuild trust and open doors to healthier, more intimate relationships. It is time to nourish your emotional centre and embrace the joy and balance you deserve. You deserve to feel happy and connected!

Worksheet 2: Forgiveness with the sacral chakra worksheet for embracing your creative flow

Write down, "Today, I honour my healing by releasing guilt and hurt with compassion. I embrace forgiveness, reclaiming my inner strength and creativity. As I plant a seed of healing, I trust it will blossom into peace and joy. This release is for my growth, happiness and freedom to create."

Affirmations for forgiveness to colour your day

- "I embrace creativity and forgiveness."

- "I let go of hurt and welcome joy."

- "I forgive myself and others with love."

Exercise 2.1: Accept what cannot be changed and emotional cleansing ritual

On Day 2, focus on accepting what cannot be changed. Reflect on the person, situation or event you acknowledged on Day 1. Allow yourself to fully feel any lingering pain, frustration or regret tied to this experience. Accept that while you cannot change the past, you can control how it affects your present. By embracing this truth, you release the emotional weight it carries, making space for peace and healing.

Find a quiet space, fill a bowl with water and add calming herbs or salt. As you dip your hands into the water, visualize your emotional pain dissolving into it. Allow the water to cleanse and renew you, symbolizing the release of what no longer serves you. This ritual connects to your sacral chakra, fostering emotional flow and forgiveness. By the end, notice the calm and emotional freedom that follows—another step forward on your journey of forgiveness.

Forgiveness and beej mantra meditation for the sacral chakra

"Vam" (pronounced "vahm" or "vum") is the mantra for the sacral chakra. Combining this mantra with inner child work creates a powerful tool for healing and self-forgiveness, making the meditation more holistic. Nurturing your inner child allows you to face past hurts and embrace emotional growth.

This meditation supports your sacral chakra while nurturing your creativity and emotional well-being. The more you connect with your inner self, the easier it becomes to release pain and open your heart to joy. Remember, you have the power to heal, and each step you take brings you closer to a life filled with love and acceptance.

- Find a cosy spot where you can sit comfortably. Close your eyes, take a deep breath and allow yourself to relax. Feel your body sink into the surface beneath you, grounding you in this moment.

- Inhale deeply, then exhale while chanting "Vam". Picture warm orange energy expanding from your sacral chakra, helping you release guilt and emotional blockages, filling you with a sense of emotional freedom and peace. Imagine this energy glowing brighter with each breath. Let the vibration resonate within you for 5–10 minutes, wrapping you in warmth and love.

- Now, visualize your younger self in your mind. See this child clearly, with their innocent eyes and gentle spirit. Spend time with this child, offering love, understanding and compassion. Wrap them in healing energy, feeling the warmth of your love surrounding them.

- As you do this, repeat the affirmation: "I embrace my inner child with love and compassion. I forgive myself for past hurts, and I allow healing to flow through me." You can say this out loud or write it down afterwards to reinforce its power.

- Gently shift your focus back to your breath. Slowly open your eyes and express gratitude for this healing time, saying, "Thank you for helping me heal and grow." Acknowledge your effort and honour your journey.

- Finally, reflect on your experience. How do you feel now? Take some time to let the effects settle in, and consider jotting down any thoughts or feelings that came up during your practice.

....

....

....

....

....

....

....

....

Yoga for the sacral chakra: Forgiveness and emotional release

Start your day with some light yoga to release tension and stimulate the sacral chakra.

Asana 2.1: Goddess Pose (Utkata Konasana)

This posture encourages emotional flow and creative expression. By opening the hips and engaging the lower body, you invite energy to flow freely, promoting a sense of empowerment and connection to your inner self.

Asana 2.2: Bound Angle Pose (Baddha Konasana)

This restorative pose opens the hips and promotes emotional release. It encourages deep breathing and relaxation, allowing you to connect with your inner child and nurture feelings of love and compassion.

Food for the sacral chakra

The foods we eat are important for our emotional health as well. For today's meals, focus on nourishing your sacral chakra with options like oranges, sweet potatoes and nuts. Oranges ignite creativity and joy, while sweet potatoes provide grounding energy. Nuts add healthy fats that help maintain emotional balance. Together, these foods create a nourishing, uplifting meal that supports your emotional well-being and encourages the free flow of feelings.

Exercise 2.2: Forgiveness exercise—heal through art

Take a moment to create a drawing or painting that reflects your emotions around forgiveness. Don't worry about making it perfect—this is your personal expression. Use colours and shapes to represent feelings like anger, guilt or release. Once done, reflect on what your art represents. This process helps you get in touch with deeper emotions you may not be fully aware of.

What feelings surfaced that you didn't expect?

……

……

……

……

……

……

……

……

……

Closing ritual : Reflect on forgiveness and healing

As you conclude Day 2, take a peaceful moment to reflect on the emotions released and the ease within your sacral chakra.

What emotions are you holding back? How could expressing them help you feel more joyful, creative and connected, leading to better relationships?

....

....

....

....

....

....

....

....

....

....

A promise to myself

Date:

Today, I took another step towards forgiveness and healing. I feel ...

....

....

....

....

....

....

....

....

....

I release the past; I embrace my creativity and emotional flow.

Remember, forgiveness doesn't happen overnight, and healing takes time. Be patient with yourself—acknowledge and accept that some things can't be changed. By releasing the past, you unlock emotional flow and healing. Each day brings you closer to feeling lighter, freer and at peace. Healing is a journey that allows your heart and spirit to embrace peace, joy and emotional freedom.

Day 3 : Forgiveness—heal and shine

"Holding on to anger is like drinking poison and expecting the other person to die."—Buddha

Are your old hurts still holding you back from truly living your life? I know that feeling; it is like a dark cloud following you, making it hard to see the sunshine. But here is the truth: *forgiveness is your key to freedom.*

It is not about saying it is okay to the person who hurt you. It is about you. It is about making the conscious choice to let go of the emotional grip those old wounds have on your heart. It is about stepping into a brighter, more joyful future, a future you truly deserve. Forgiveness takes real courage to let go. When you forgive, you are reclaiming your life and your power. You are creating space within yourself for healing and growth.

Holding on to anger and bitterness steals your joy. Research shows that forgiveness is strongly linked to higher self-esteem. It helps reduce feelings like anger and despair, and makes way for hope, confidence and a stronger sense of self.

Unleash your inner sun

Your solar plexus chakra is like your personal powerhouse of confidence. It is connected to your ability to forgive. When it is balanced, you feel confident and full of energy. But when you hold on to resentment, it blocks that energy. You might feel lost and powerless.

Forgiveness unlocks your strength, putting you in control of your emotions.

You deserve confidence, peace and true healing. Releasing past burdens unlocks your power to heal, grow and live fully.

Worksheet 3: Forgiveness with the solar plexus chakra worksheet for igniting your inner light

Write down, "Today, I focus on my solar plexus chakra, releasing resentment and pain that have weighed me down. I reclaim my strength, allowing the light of forgiveness to fill me with courage.

I choose to let go and move forward, trusting in my power to heal and shine."

Affirmations for forgiveness to empower your day

- "I let go of fear and doubts, feeling strong and free."
- "I embrace my power and choose forgiveness."
- "With every breath, I release anger and welcome healing."

Exercise 3.1: Recognize the cost of holding on—ignite your inner flame

On Day 3, after acknowledging your pain (Day 1) and accepting what cannot be changed (Day 2), it is time to face the true cost of holding on to anger, resentment and fear. These emotions drain your energy and block your growth. Today, reflect on the specific person, event or situation you have been focusing on, and how these unresolved feelings have affected your emotional and mental well-being. Consider how holding on to these emotions has impacted your peace, happiness and personal strength. Write down your fears and doubts on a piece of paper and reflect on what keeping them has cost you in terms of freedom and inner power.

Once ready, burn the paper. As the flames rise, imagine your fears turning to ash, leaving you lighter and more empowered. This ritual, tied to the solar plexus chakra, represents personal power and transformation. Releasing these emotions allows you to reclaim your power and begin healing. Remember, forgiveness is not just about letting go of others; it is also about forgiving yourself and making space for the vibrant person you are meant to be.

Forgiveness and beej mantra meditation for the solar plexus chakra

"Ram" (pronounced " rahm" or "rum") is the mantra for the solar plexus chakra. When you combine this mantra with Inner Fire Meditation, you create a powerful tool for releasing emotional blockages and fostering self-empowerment. The "Ram" mantra helps align and energize your solar plexus, while invoking a sense of courage and self-worth. Together, they pave the way for forgiveness and a deeper connection to your authentic self.

- Find a quiet place where you can sit comfortably and feel at ease. Take a deep breath in, inviting positive energy and exhale any tension or negativity that you may be carrying.

- Inhale deeply, and as you exhale, chant "Ram". Visualize a warm golden light radiating from your solar plexus chakra, located just above your navel. This light helps release feelings of shame and fear, filling you with confidence and a sense of personal empowerment. With each breath, imagine this energy growing brighter and stronger, enveloping you in warmth and love.

- Imagine a vibrant fire at your solar plexus, burning away everything that no longer serves you. This fire symbolizes the transformation you seek, releasing past hurts and limiting beliefs into ashes. Fire fuels movement and action in your life, turning your intentions into reality. When your inner flame burns brightly, it empowers you to pursue your passions and express your true self in the world.

- Now, repeat this affirmation—"I release all doubts and embrace my strength and the power of forgiveness. I am worthy of success and happiness." Say it aloud or write it down to reinforce its impact.

- Slowly, shift your focus back to your breath. When you are ready, gently open your eyes and express gratitude for this healing time, saying, "Thank you for helping me reclaim my power."

- Let the effects settle in and consider jotting down any thoughts or feelings that arose during your practice. This reflection can deepen your understanding and support your ongoing journey of healing and empowerment.

Yoga for the solar plexus chakra: Forgiveness and emotional release

Start your day with some light yoga to release tension and stimulate the sacral chakra.

Asana 3.1: Boat Pose (Navasana)

This pose strengthens the core and promotes confidence, helping you connect with your personal power.

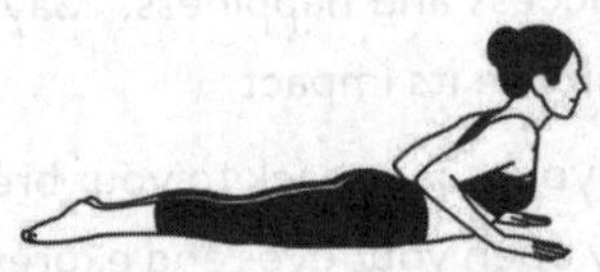

Asana 3.2: Cobra Pose (Bhujangasana)

This heart-opening pose can help release emotional tension and foster feelings of forgiveness and compassion in you.

Food for the solar plexus chakra

Nourish your body with foods that uplift your emotional health. Today, focus on foods like yellow bell peppers, quinoa and chickpeas. Yellow bell peppers embody joy and warmth, while quinoa and chickpeas offer grounding energy and strength. Together, these nourishing foods support your journey towards emotional well-being and foster your ability to forgive and embrace your true self.

Exercise 3.2: Reflect and shift your perspective

This exercise encourages self-reflection and empathy by examining a painful experience. It invites you to explore your emotions and how the situation affected your self-esteem, and its impact on your relationships. Be honest with yourself and let your feelings flow freely. Additionally, it encourages viewing the situation from the other person's perspective to promote understanding, compassion and emotional healing.

Write down that specific hurtful event.

… …

… …

....

....

....

....

....

....

....

....

How did this event make you feel about yourself? Did you experience feelings of embarrassment, unworthiness, betrayal, frustration, sadness, anger or powerlessness?

....

....

....

....

....

....

....

....

....

How has this event influenced your thoughts and behaviour? What specific patterns do you notice in your feelings or actions since then? For example, have you become more cautious, withdrawn or reactive?

... ...

... ...

... ...

... ...

... ...

... ...

... ...

Imagine the life of the person who hurt you. What struggles they might have faced? This is not to excuse their actions, but to foster empathy and understanding.

... ...

... ...

... ...

... ...

... ...

....

....

....

....

....

This awareness can help foster compassion within you. Now, visualize yourself letting go of any anger and resentment, allowing space for healing and peace.

Closing ritual: Reflect on forgiveness and healing

As you conclude Day 3, take a peaceful moment to reflect on the emotions released and the ease within your solar plexus chakra.

What beliefs or doubts make you feel weak or insecure?

....

....

....

....

....

....

....

....

How can you let them go to embrace your true strength?

....

....

....

....

....

....

....

....

....

A promise to myself

Date:

Today, I took a meaningful step towards forgiveness and healing. I feel ...

....

....

....

....

....

....

....

....

....

....

I release the past; I embrace my inner strength and personal power.

Remember, forgiveness is a journey, not a destination. Healing unfolds with time, so be gentle with yourself. You deserve to shine and embrace a life filled with joy.

Day 4 : Forgiveness—transition from grudges to growth

"Forgiveness is not just a blessing you give to another person. It's a gift you give to yourself."—Marianne Williamson

Want to break the invisible wall between you and someone you care about? It is a painful barrier that builds up over time, causing misunderstandings and lingering conflicts, which gradually fade the warmth in your relationship.

Forgiveness is incredibly powerful. When you choose to forgive, you start tearing down those walls, opening your heart in ways you might not have believed possible. This creates space for new experiences, allowing you to connect with others on a deeper level and inviting more compassion and understanding into your life.

Studies show that forgiving lights up areas of our brains linked to empathy, helping us feel more connected and find deeper peace within ourselves.

Letting go of the past isn't just about feeling lighter; it is about embracing others with newfound openness. Choosing forgiveness means choosing to live with a more joyful and full heart—it is a true gift to yourself.

Unblock the heart through forgiveness

The heart chakra is our centre of love, compassion and forgiveness, closely tied to our ability to let go of past hurts. When balanced, we feel open and free, forgiving easily and fostering deeper connections that fill our lives with warmth and joy.

In contrast, an imbalanced heart chakra brings heaviness, leading us to hold on to grudges and let anger fester. It feels like being trapped behind a wall, making it hard to reach out to loved ones and leaving us feeling isolated. However, we can heal our heart chakra through forgiveness, choosing to open our hearts and release pain, ultimately creating space for joy and connection once again.

Worksheet 4: Forgiveness with the heart chakra worksheet for opening the heart

Write down, "Today, I open my heart to forgiveness, releasing the pain that has been holding me back. I choose to heal, embracing love and compassion for myself and others. With each breath, I invite peace and understanding, knowing that opening my heart leads to freedom. Today, I trust in the power of healing and connection."

Affirmations for forgiveness to infuse love into your day

- "I welcome love and choose forgiveness with every breath."
- "I release negativity and embrace compassion for myself and others."
- "With each moment, I nurture joy and deepen my connections."

Exercise 4.1: See things from their perspective—a hug to heal

On Day 4, after acknowledging your pain (Day 1), accepting what cannot be changed (Day 2) and recognizing the cost of holding on (Day 3), it is time to embrace healing through the heart. Hugging, a simple yet powerful act, helps release emotional tension and invites peace. Today, focus on the person or event you are working to forgive. Imagine hugging them—not to justify their actions, but to understand their humanity. Consider what they may have been going through and how their actions were shaped by their own struggles. By seeing things from their perspective, you allow yourself to release anger and frustration, making room for healing.

Also, today, hug your loved ones—family and friends and picture a soft green light radiating from your heart. With each squeeze, let go of anger, resentment and pain, allowing yourself to release what no longer serves you. Hugging not only opens the heart but also releases feel-good chemicals, bringing you peace. After each hug, pause and reflect—how do you feel? This practice brings you closer to emotional freedom and inner peace.

Forgiveness and beej mantra meditation for the heart chakra

The mantra "Yam" (pronounced "yahm" or "yum") is associated with the heart chakra. Combining this mantra with anahata forgiveness practice meditation creates a powerful practice for healing, forgiveness and restoring emotional balance. The Yam mantra aligns and energizes your heart chakra, while anahata forgiveness practice helps release negative emotions. Together, they open the path to deep emotional healing and renewed connections.

- To begin, find a quiet place where you can sit comfortably. Close your eyes and take a few deep breaths to centre yourself.

- Start by chanting or silently repeating the mantra "Yam". Focus on your heart chakra, located at the centre of your chest. As you repeat "Yam", imagine a warm green light expanding from your heart, filling your body with love and compassion. Let this light release any tension or emotional heaviness you may be holding on to. Continue this for 2–3 minutes.

- Next, move into the four anahata forgiveness practice phrases: softly say or think, "I'm sorry", "Please forgive me", "Thank you" and "I love you." To deepen this practice, visualize the person in front of you and make eye contact in your mind, feeling the connection and sincerity behind each phrase:

"I'm sorry": Acknowledge your role in the hurt or conflict and take responsibility.

"Please forgive me": Sincerely seek forgiveness from others and yourself.

"Thank you": Express gratitude for the lessons and growth the experience has brought.

"I love you": Let love flow freely, visualizing peace, healing and reconnection.

- After the anahata forgiveness practice phrases, return to focusing on your breath, feeling the peace of letting go. Slowly open your eyes and express gratitude by saying, "Thank you for helping me heal".

- Take a moment to reflect on your feelings. Consider writing down any insights or emotions that arose during the meditation.

Yoga for the heart chakra: Forgiveness and emotional release

Start your day with some light yoga to release tension and stimulate your heart chakra.

Asana 4.1: Camel Pose (Ustrasana)

This opens your heart centre, releasing stored emotions and fostering vulnerability.

Asana 4.2: Bridge Pose (Setu Bandhasana)

This gentle backbend activates your heart chakra, allowing space for emotional healing.

Food for the heart chakra

Nourish your heart chakra and emotional well-being with foods that promote healing and forgiveness. Focus on green, heart-centred foods like leafy greens, avocado, cucumber and green tea. These foods help balance your heart chakra, encouraging love and compassion.

Leafy greens like spinach and kale foster emotional healing and bring a sense of inner calm. Avocado supports the heart with its healthy fats, promoting self-love and emotional resilience. Together, these foods work to open your heart, helping you release past hurts and embrace forgiveness. Let your meals be a part of your healing journey, supporting your ability to let go and invite love and peace into your life.

Exercise 4.2: Swadhyaya (self-reflection)

To practice forgiveness and reflect on your heart chakra, try the swadhyaya (self-reflection) exercise. This practice promotes empathy, compassion and a deeper understanding of your relationships. It opens your heart and enhances emotional connections, helping you forgive and grow. Reflect on these three questions, focusing on a specific person, relationship, or event:

What have you received from this person? Consider the support, love or lessons they have provided you.

… …

… …

… …

… …

… …

… …

… …

… …

What have you given to this person? Think about the help, love or time you have shared with them.

… …

… …

… …

… …

… …

… …

....

....

....

What troubles or difficulties have you caused this person? Acknowledge any hurtful actions or words that may have affected them.

....

....

....

....

....

....

....

....

....

These self-reflection exercises are based on the Naikan technique—a Japanese practice that uses the same questions to reflect on different themes like forgiveness and gratitude. This method encourages you to look deeply at your experiences, recognize patterns in your relationships, and gain insight into your own thoughts and feelings. By revisiting the same questions with different focuses, you gradually develop greater self-awareness, compassion and understanding.

"We do not learn from experience... we learn from reflecting on experience."—John Dewey

Take a moment to sit with your thoughts and feelings. Consider what these reflections reveal about your patterns, responses and personal growth.

What new understanding or awareness did you gain through this reflection?

....

....

....

....

....

....

....

....

Closing ritual: Reflect on forgiveness and healing

As you conclude Day 4, take a peaceful moment to reflect on the emotions released and the ease within your heart chakra.

What behaviours of yours might upset others?

………

………

………

………

………

………

………

………

………

………

What actions can you take to improve or heal those relationships?

………

………

………

………

………

………

………

... ...

... ...

A promise to myself

Date:

Today, I took a significant step towards forgiveness and healing. I feel...

... ...

... ...

... ...

... ...

... ...

... ...

... ...

... ...

I release the past; I open my heart to love and compassion.

Remember, when you let go of resentment, you become more empathetic, fostering stronger connections with others. Understanding others' perspectives deepens this empathy, creating a positive cycle of healthier interactions. This leads to building a supportive network, strengthening relationships, and promoting mutual respect, compassion and understanding.

Day 5 : Forgiveness—rebuild trust, restore harmony

"The weak can never forgive. Forgiveness is the attribute of the strong."—Mahatma Gandhi

Let me share a story about my client, Arjun. He was a loving person who believed in love and trust. His relationship with his girlfriend filled him with joy and dreams for the future, but everything changed when he discovered her betrayal. This shattered his heart, leaving him angry and confused. The hurt consumed him, stealing his sleep and filling his days with worry. Arjun realized that holding on to this pain was only hurting him more, so he longed for peace and took a step towards healing.

One powerful exercise I recommended was writing an unsent letter to his ex-girlfriend. This was about confronting the emotions he had carried inside rather than sending it. As Arjun wrote, he began to see his ex-girlfriend as a person who made mistakes instead of just being the source of his suffering. This shift helped him cultivate empathy and recognize her struggles. I reminded him that forgiveness is a conscious choice to let go of negativity and embrace self-compassion. Healing is possible, and he is worthy of peace.

Unlock forgiveness through expression

The throat chakra is our centre for communication and plays a crucial role in forgiveness. When balanced, we can share our feelings openly, essential for healing and understanding. However, when it is imbalanced, expressing emotions can become difficult, leading to unresolved feelings and resentment. By nurturing our throat chakra, we empower ourselves to speak our truth, allowing forgiveness to flow and deepening our connections with others.

Forgiveness begins with acknowledging your feelings—hurt, anger or sadness. It is perfectly normal to experience these emotions. Once you recognize them, it is important to express how you feel. You might write it down, speak it aloud or share it. This expression creates a healing path. As you let go of negativity, you open the door to empathy and gain insight into the other person's perspective. You deserve peace and joy. I believe in your strength to heal.

Worksheet 5: Forgiveness with the throat chakra worksheet for empowering expression

Write down, "Today, I honour the power of my voice to heal and release. By speaking my truth, I allow my throat chakra to flow freely, clearing the space for forgiveness. I choose to express my feelings honestly, whether through writing or speaking, knowing that this is the path to inner peace. In this moment, I give myself the permission to let go of pain and open up to healing."

Affirmations for forgiveness to heal connection

- "I speak my truth with love and forgiveness."

- "My voice is strong, clear and free from resentment."

- "I express my feelings openly and choose to forgive."

Exercise 5.1: Forgive yourself—reclaim your inner voice

On Day 5, after acknowledging your pain (Day 1), accepting what can't be changed (Day 2), recognizing the impact of holding on (Day 3) and embracing empathy (Day 4), it is time for self-forgiveness. Release the guilt, regret and pain you have been carrying by acknowledging your imperfections and letting go of self-judgement. Start by speaking about your emotions aloud to someone you trust or to yourself in the mirror. Then, write a letter of forgiveness to yourself, expressing your regrets and letting go of blame.

When finished, read the letter, tear it up and discard it— symbolizing the release of those heavy emotions. Reflect on how it feels to recognize your mistakes without self-criticism. Notice the relief that comes from letting go and the space it creates for growth. This act of forgiveness invites inner peace and opens the heart to new possibilities. Take a deep breath and feel the lightness and clarity that comes with this step towards healing.

Forgiveness and beej mantra meditation for the throat chakra

This throat chakra meditation is a simple yet powerful way to connect with your true voice and foster forgiveness within yourself. By chanting the mantra "Ham" (pronounced "hahm" or "hum"), you can help balance and calm your throat chakra, allowing clear and peaceful expression.

- Find a peaceful, comfortable place where you can sit undisturbed. Sit with your spine straight, close your eyes and rest your hands on your lap. Take a few deep breaths, letting your body and mind settle.

- As you inhale deeply, exhale with a gentle chant of "Ham". You can whisper it or say it aloud—whatever feels right for you. Picture a clear, blue light forming in your throat, open and calm like the sky. With each breath, feel this light expanding, opening your throat chakra and releasing your truth. Allow yourself to relax into this space, feeling free to let your true feelings flow.

- Keep breathing into this light, allowing it to glow brighter with each exhale. Let the vibration fill you, wrapping you in peace and warmth. If emotions arise, know that it is okay; this is part of your healing.

- Think about why you are here—maybe to release pain, to forgive or to find your voice. Hold on to this intention as you breathe; it is your anchor. Now, try saying the affirmation: "I am free to express myself and let go of the past." Speak it softly or write it down to strengthen its impact.

- Sit quietly for a few more moments, letting the energy settle within you. Feel calmness and clarity in your heart.

- When you are ready, take a deep breath, come back to the present and reflect on how you feel. Notice any lightness or peace that fills you, and carry this healing as you move forward. You have the strength to heal and each step brings you closer.

Yoga for the throat chakra: Forgiveness and emotional release

Start your day with gentle yoga to release tension and open up the throat chakra.

Asana 5.1: Lion's Breath (Simhasana)

This powerful breathwork clears your throat chakra, allowing you to vocalize your feelings and release negativity.

Asana 5.2: Fish Pose (Matsyasana)

This pose opens your throat, creating a sense of freedom in expressing your truth and fostering forgiveness.

Food for the throat chakra

Nourish your throat chakra and emotional health with foods that promote healing and forgiveness. Focus on blue and purple foods like blueberries, blackberries and purple grapes. These delicious options help balance your throat chakra, inviting love and compassion into your life.

Blueberries are full of antioxidants, which can bring emotional balance and calm. Blackberries are rich in vitamins that support your throat chakra, helping you express your feelings more clearly.

Let these foods support your healing journey, helping you release past hurts and embrace love and peace.

Exercise 5.2: The empowering letter

Writing a forgiveness letter is a great way to share your feelings and start healing. Putting your emotions into words helps you let go of anger and move towards forgiveness.

Find a piece of paper and write to someone who has hurt you. In your letter, tell them you forgive them for what they did. Use "I" statements to explain how their actions affected you, like "I felt hurt when …" This helps you express your feelings clearly.

Also, think about their struggles. Consider any difficulties they might have faced. This can help you feel more understanding and compassionate. Next, reflect on your own journey. How has holding on to this pain affected your life? Recognize that you want to heal and let go. End your letter on a positive note. Say something like, "I choose to release this hurt and move forward."

To close the process, create a small ritual. Read the letter out loud, as if you are speaking to that person. Then tear it up and let the pieces go—either throw them away or let them drift in the air. This shows you are releasing the burden. Afterwards, take a moment to think about these questions:

What made you decide to write this letter to that person? How did you feel before?

What changes do you notice in your feelings now that you have expressed forgiveness?

This process can help you let go of negative emotions and welcome healing and peace into your life. Take it step by step—you have the strength to heal.

Closing ritual: Reflect on forgiveness and healing

As you conclude Day 5, take a peaceful moment to reflect on the emotions released and the ease within your throat chakra.

What words or ways of speaking might upset others?

....

....

....

....

....

....

....

....

How can you positively improve strained relationships?

....

....

....

....

… …

… …

… …

… …

… …

A promise to myself

Date:

Today, I took an important step towards forgiveness and healing. I feel …

… …

… …

… …

… …

… …

… …

… …

… …

… …

I release the past; I open my throat to clear communication and forgiveness.

Remember, forgiveness begins with expressing your truth and letting go of what no longer serves you. While forgiving others is vital, self-forgiveness is equally important. It frees you from past guilt, allowing compassion and inner peace to grow. Embrace the journey, express yourself and make space for healing and growth.

Day 6 : Forgiveness—unlock peace

"Forgiveness is not an occasional act; it is a constant attitude."
—Martin Luther King Jr

Have you ever felt a tight knot of anger in your chest? It can feel like a storm inside you, draining your energy and joy. But what if I told you that you have the power to calm that storm?

Forgiveness isn't about saying that what happened was okay; it is about choosing your own peace. When you forgive, your brain shifts gears. You activate your prefrontal cortex, the part that helps you think clearly and make better decisions. This shift allows you to process your emotions in a healthier way, turning conflicts into opportunities for growth. You will find yourself understanding others more deeply, which opens your heart to compassion and empathy.

Forgiveness also soothes your amygdala, the part of your brain that stirs up anger and stress. When you practise empathy, you soften those feelings of resentment. This journey is about finding emotional strength and freedom.

Open the mind's eye

Forgiveness is closely tied to your third eye chakra, the centre of intuition and understanding. When you practise forgiveness, you open your mind to new perspectives. This helps you see situations clearly and compassionately, leading to emotional balance.

But when you hold on to grudges, your third eye chakra can become blocked, creating confusion and fear. You may struggle to trust your instincts or see the truth in your relationships. Embracing forgiveness allows you to release those heavy feelings, clearing your mind and heart. Together, let's choose forgiveness and welcome clarity and peace into our lives.

Worksheet 6: Forgiveness with the third eye chakra worksheet for awakening inner clarity

"Today, I observe my emotions without judgment, embracing them with compassion and clarity. I release old guilt and pain, inviting the wisdom of forgiveness and self-understanding. Nurturing my inner peace and intuition, I trust that this clarity will grow, allowing me to live fully in the present—free and open."

Affirmations for forgiveness to awaken inner clarity

- "I welcome clarity and let go of the past."

- "I release old patterns and open to understanding."

- "With each breath, I find peace and wisdom."

Exercise 6.1: Set an intention to forgive

On Day 5, after acknowledging your pain (Day 1), accepting what cannot be changed (Day 2), recognizing the cost of holding on to the past (Day 3), embracing empathy (Day 4) and self-forgiveness (Day 5) it is time to set an intention to forgive. Start by imagining the person or an incident that you are working to forgive, sitting across from an empty chair. Speak openly and honestly, expressing forgiveness or asking for it. Once you have shared your heart, switch chairs and take a deep breath, imagining their perspective—consider their thoughts, feelings and experiences. Connect with your third eye chakra for clarity, visualizing an indigo light clearing confusion and guiding your healing. By setting this intention, you release emotional blockages and invite peace into your life. Reflect on the insights you have gained and how they can help you move forward. You have taken a powerful step in releasing the past, creating space for peace, growth and emotional freedom.

Forgiveness and beej mantra meditation for the third eye chakra

The mantra "Om" (pronounced AUM) is associated with the third eye chakra, a powerful focal point for intuition and insight. When combined with trataka meditation, it becomes a transformative practice for healing and forgiveness. The Om mantra aligns and energizes your third eye, while trataka enhances your mental focus, allowing for profound emotional release and clarity.

- Find a quiet, comfortable place to sit. Light a candle and position it at eye level, about an arm's length away. This flame will be your point of focus for trataka meditation. As you inhale, invite positive energy into your being, and as you exhale, release tension and negativity.

- Gaze softly at the candle flame without blinking for about 2 minutes, allowing its warmth and light to envelop you.

After this, close your eyes and hold the mental image of the flame for an additional 3 minutes, connecting to the peace it brings.

- Allow the flame to draw you deeper into your practice. Now, shift your attention to your third eye chakra, located between your eyebrows. Inhale deeply, and as you exhale, begin chanting "Om". Repeat the mantra silently or aloud for 2–3 minutes. Visualize a soothing indigo light expanding from your third eye chakra, releasing doubt and inviting clarity. With each breath, feel this light growing brighter, resonating within you for 4–5 minutes, wrapping you in warmth and healing.

- After your mantra practice, repeat the affirmation, "I release all burdens and embrace my inner wisdom and the power of forgiveness. I am worthy of clarity and peace." Speak it aloud or write it down to reinforce its meaning in your heart.

- Slowly bring your focus back to your breath. When you feel ready, gently open your eyes and express gratitude for this healing moment by saying, "Thank you for helping me see with clarity."

- Allow the effects of your meditation to settle within you. Consider jotting down any insights or feelings that emerged during your practice, as this can deepen your healing journey and keep your intentions clear.

Yoga for the third eye chakra: Forgiveness and emotional release

Begin your day with soothing yoga to invite forgiveness and activate the third eye chakra, encouraging self-awareness and inner peace.

Asana 6.1: Shoulder Stand (Sarvangasana)

This pose energizes the third eye, helping clear mental blocks and encouraging a forgiving mindset.

Asana 6.2: Forward Bend (Uttanasana)

This asana promotes deep introspection, grounding and emotional release, fostering a sense of understanding and compassion.

Food for third eye chakra

Support your third eye chakra and emotional well-being with foods that invite insight and release. Enjoy purple and blue foods like blueberries, plums and purple grapes. These foods aid in balancing the third eye chakra, fostering forgiveness and enhancing clarity.

Blueberries, high in antioxidants, offer a calming effect that supports emotional balance. Plums and purple grapes, rich in nutrients, nourish the mind, helping you see things more clearly and let go of the past. Embrace these healing foods as part of your journey to clarity, self-compassion and inner peace.

Exercise 6.2: Claim your power

Choose one person or situation to forgive and acknowledge your feelings. Facing difficult emotions is crucial for healing and moving forward.

List what happened and how you were hurt.

…… ……/ ……

…… ……

…… ……

…… ……

…… ……

…… ……

…… ……

··

··

Is holding on to this grudge benefitting you in any way?

··

··

··

··

··

··

··

··

Forgiveness can be challenging, especially when feelings of revenge or anger arise. Writing down your emotions, including any desire for revenge, can be a powerful way to release those feelings. It allows you to let go of the pain that holds you back, instead of letting it control you. Visualize the person who hurt you and write down everything you want to say or do to them—express yourself fully without holding back. This practice helps you process and release the emotions, promoting healing and emotional freedom.

… …

… …

… …

… …

… …

… …

… …

… …

… …

You can't control others, but you can control how you respond. Holding on to anger or blame keeps you stuck in the past. Choose to release the pain and forgive—not for the other person, but for your own peace, so you can move forward.

What actions or mindset will you adopt to let go and avoid hurting yourself again?

… …

… …

… …

… …

… …

… …

... ...

... ...

... ...

Closing ritual: Reflect on forgiveness and healing

As you conclude Day 6, take a peaceful moment to reflect on the emotions released and the ease within your third eye chakra.

What thought patterns in your daily life prevent you from seeking forgiveness?

... ...

... ...

... ...

... ...

... ...

... ...

... ...

... ...

... ...

How can you change them?

... ...

... ...

A promise to myself

Date:

Today, I took a profound step towards forgiveness and healing. I feel ...

I release the past; I open my mind to clarity and intuition.

Remember, the feeling of revenge blocks forgiveness, but releasing it can bring real change. Write down everything you want to say or do in anger and then destroy the paper. Studies in neuroscience show that the brain often responds similarly to imagined or symbolic actions as it does to real experiences. When you vividly express or visualize an emotion—such as anger, grief or forgiveness—the same neural pathways activate as if the event were actually taking place. This is why symbolic acts like writing and then destroying a letter can bring a genuine sense of release and emotional relief. Forgiveness calms the neural networks controlling stress, pain and threat awareness, lowering stress hormones, and improving both physical and mental health. Thus, helping you heal.

Day 7 : Forgiveness—stay on the path to personal growth

> "We win by tenderness. We conquer by forgiveness."
> —Frederick William Robertson

You might wonder, *Does forgiving someone mean I'm saying what they did is okay? Am I supposed to act like nothing happened?* This raises an important point: forgiveness is not the same as forgetting. While forgiving can free us from emotional burdens, forgetting isn't always possible. Instead, we can acknowledge the past and choose to move forward without being weighed down by it.

In addition to forgiving others, it is crucial to forgive ourselves. Often, we are our own harshest critics, replaying our mistakes in our minds. Just as you would forgive a friend for their missteps, you deserve that same kindness. Remember, we are all human and learning together. It is perfectly okay to let go of our past mistakes.

Forgiving yourself is a powerful step towards personal growth. It means recognizing that you did your best with what you knew at the time. Now, you are evolving into a better version of yourself, and that is something to embrace.

Embrace forgiveness for spiritual connection

Forgiveness is deeply connected to your crown chakra, the centre of spiritual connection and higher consciousness. When you practise forgiveness, you open yourself to a greater understanding of yourself and others. This shift fosters a sense of peace and unity, allowing you to transcend negativity and experience emotional healing.

Conversely, holding on to grudges can block your crown chakra, leading to feelings of disconnection and isolation. This imbalance may cause confusion about your purpose and hinder your ability to tap into your inner wisdom. By embracing forgiveness, you release the burdens of resentment, allowing your spirit to flourish and your connection to the universe to deepen.

When we forgive, we open the door to a higher state of awareness and spiritual harmony.

Worksheet 7: Forgiveness with the crown chakra worksheet for embracing spiritual clarity

"Today, I open myself to observe my emotions with love and understanding, allowing clarity to flow through me. I release past guilt and pain, welcoming the wisdom that forgiveness brings. As I deepen my spiritual connection, I trust that clarity will grow, offering acceptance and peace. This journey of forgiveness is a sacred gift for my freedom and wholeness."

Affirmations for forgiveness and enlightenment

- "I embrace love and let go of what no longer serves me."
- "I choose forgiveness to open my heart and mind."
- "I connect with my higher self, inviting peace and clarity into my life."

Exercise 7.1: Release and let go—writing an unsent letter of forgiveness

On Day 7, after acknowledging your pain (Days 1–3), choosing empathy (Day 4) and forgiving yourself (Day 5) and setting intention (Day 6), it is time to fully release what no longer serves you. Write a heartfelt letter to the person or about the event, expressing your emotions—anger, sadness and any lingering resentment. Be honest. As you write, focus on forgiving the person, acknowledging their actions and letting go of the hold they have had on you. Clearly state what you have learned from the experience and how it has shaped you. Once finished, destroy the letter—tear it or burn it—to symbolically release the past. This act signifies your conscious decision to prioritize peace and growth over past pain. Feel the freedom as you create space for healing, clarity and a brighter future, untethered from old wounds. While Exercise 6.2 guides you to acknowledge and release anger, Exercise 7.1 helps you find closure through forgiveness.

Forgiveness and beej mantra meditation for the crown chakra

This meditation focuses on the crown chakra, which connects you to your higher self and the universe. It fosters forgiveness, allowing you to release past burdens and embrace inner peace.

- Begin by finding a quiet, comfortable space to sit undisturbed. Close your eyes and take a few deep breaths to center yourself.

- Start chanting or silently repeating the mantra "Om". The third eye and crown chakras are associated with spiritual connection and intuition, and "Om" resonates with them. Focus on your crown chakra at the top of your head and visualize a warm, violet light radiating from this area. With each repetition of "Om", imagine this light expanding, filling your body with compassion and understanding. Allow it to dissolve any feelings of anger or resentment. Continue this for 2–3 minutes.

- As you breathe in deeply, direct your attention to the violet chakra. Visualize a magnificent white lotus with closed petals at the centre of your crown chakra. Observe its shape, colour and texture. As you concentrate, see the lotus slowly spinning and its petals beginning to open one by one.

- With each petal that opens, feel the energy of forgiveness flowing through you. The lotus blooms, revealing layers of petals that symbolize the endless journey of forgiveness and growth. Imagine your crown chakra spinning harmoniously with the lotus, its violet light enveloping you and connecting you to the universe.

- Breathe deeply, embracing the energy that flows from above and below, uniting you with all that exists.

- When you are ready, gently open your eyes. Repeat the affirmation, "I release all burdens and embrace my inner wisdom and the power of forgiveness. I am worthy of clarity and peace." Speak it aloud or write it down to reinforce its meaning.

- As you settle back into your breath, express gratitude for this healing moment by saying, "Thank you for helping me see with clarity." Allow the effects of your meditation to settle, and take a moment to jot down any insights or feelings that arose during your practice.

Yoga for the crown chakra: Forgiveness and emotional release

Begin your day with calming yoga to release tension and open your crown chakra.

Asana 7.1: Lotus Pose (Padmasana)

Sit cross-legged with hands on your knees. Close your eyes and visualize a soft light above your head, inviting peace and forgiveness into your mind. Feel the gentle warmth of this light, connecting you to a sense of higher understanding.

Asana 7.2: Corpse Pose (Shavasana)

Lie on your back with arms relaxed at your sides, palms open. Let go of all tension, allowing yourself to feel fully at ease and receptive to universal energy. Embrace the stillness as you connect with inner peace and forgiveness.

Food for the crown chakra

Support your crown chakra and emotional healing with foods that encourage forgiveness and inner peace. Embrace nourishing white and violet foods like cauliflower, coconut and purple cabbage. These calming foods harmonize with your crown chakra, promoting release and fostering a gentle sense of clarity.

Coconut, with its natural soothing properties, offers emotional comfort, while purple cabbage and cauliflower provide vital nutrients that uplift your mind and spirit. Allow these mindful bites to help you release old hurts and invite serenity, supporting your journey towards forgiveness, self-compassion and a peaceful heart. Mindful eating means paying full attention to the experience of eating—savouring each bite, noticing the flavours, textures and how your body feels. Allow these mindful bites to help you release old hurts and invite serenity, supporting your journey towards forgiveness, self-compassion and a peaceful heart.

Exercise 7.2: Rewrite memories

Find a quiet, comfortable space where you won't be disturbed. Close your eyes and take a few deep breaths to relax. Visualize three significant events from your life that upset you—one from your childhood, one from your teenage or early adult years and one more recent. Picture each of these events as if they are written on a chalkboard in front of you.

Hold an eraser in your hand and gently wipe each memory away, clearing the board. Once the memory is gone, rewrite it on the board in a way that feels healing to you—transform it into a positive or peaceful memory. Focus on one memory at a time and complete it before moving to the next.

This exercise helps you to mentally rewrite past experiences, giving you the power to change how you feel about them. By doing so, you release emotional tension and shift from hurt to healing. Allow yourself to feel lighter and more at peace as you move forward with a positive outlook.

Do you still feel the same emotions, or do they feel lighter?

....

....

....

What insights have you gained from this process?

....

....

....

....

....

....

....

How can you apply them to your current life?

....

....

....

....

....

....

....

....

....

....

Closing ritual: Reflecting on forgiveness and healing

It is Day 7, you have come a long way. Take a peaceful moment to reflect on the emotions released and the ease within your crown chakra.

A promise to myself

Date:

After letting go of resentment, anger and regret and practising self-compassion for a week, do you feel lighter, more peaceful, and more open to forgiveness? What lessons have you learned? What past mistakes will you avoid in the future?

....

....

....

....

....

....

… …
… …
… …

I release all attachments; I open my mind to universal love and guidance.

Remember, forgiveness is an ongoing journey, not a one-time act. It is a powerful tool for healing, growth and self-discovery. Embracing forgiveness—both for others and yourself—releases resentment, anger and regret fosters peace and opens the door to personal transformation. By practising self-forgiveness, you unlock new opportunities for emotional freedom and personal growth. Embrace this process and watch it lead to a life filled with peace and joy.

Congratulations on completing Week 1

You have taken a step towards a more peaceful and joyful life.

Take a moment to truly appreciate how far you have come. You have shown incredible courage by facing your emotions and committing to your own healing. This isn't easy work, but you have taken the first step, and that is something to be proud of. You have given yourself the gift of growth, and you are learning to free your heart from the weight of old wounds.

As you move forward, remember that forgiveness is not just an act; it is a way of living. When you forgive others, you release the burden of resentment, and when you forgive yourself, you open the door to self-compassion. Each time you let go of the past, you create space for peace, love and light to enter your life.

Keep this in mind—true peace comes from within. Letting go is how you free yourself to live fully, with a heart that is no longer tied to pain, but open to joy and new beginnings. You are stronger than your past, and every step you take towards forgiveness is a step towards a more peaceful, fulfilled life.

"When you forgive, you in no way change the past – but you sure do change the future."—Bernard Meltzer

What are your key takeaways from this week?

WEEK 2

7 ••⦁••• Gratitude—Embrace the Present

"Gratitude can transform common days into thanksgivings, turn routine jobs into joy and change ordinary opportunities into blessings."
—William Arthur Ward

As we enter Week 2, take a moment to fully immerse yourself in the present. Gratitude will be your anchor, helping you see the beauty around you—whether it is a warm cup of tea, a loved one's laughter or the peace of nature. These little moments are gifts that nourish your soul. When you practise gratitude, you open your heart and create a ripple of joy that flows through your life.

This week's activities take only about 45 minutes to an hour, and you can spread them out to fit your day. As you commit to these practices, you will start to notice your thoughts shift and your outlook brighten. These exercises are not just for now; they are tools to use whenever you need clarity. Let this book be your guide and companion on this journey, supporting you far beyond the 21 days.

Embrace each moment with kindness to yourself. Celebrate every small step forward and honour the courage it takes to change. You are not just changing your mindset; you are reshaping your reality. Your mindset is the foundation of your destiny—build it with courage. With each moment of gratitude, you invite more abundance, love and positivity into your life.

Each day is a fresh opportunity. Trust that you are moving closer to the life you desire. Your journey is unique, and every step, no matter how small, is a victory. Embrace the process and believe in your ability to change. You are becoming the best version of yourself, one step at a time. Congratulations on making it this far—keep going. The best is yet to come.

Day 8 : Gratitude—the key to unlocking hidden happiness

"Gratitude turns what we have into enough."—Aesop

When was the last time you felt truly content? When did you pause, take a deep breath and appreciate everything you have? It is so easy to get caught up in chasing more—a better job, a bigger home, the latest gadget. We often focus on what is next and forget to live in the present. But what if the happiness we are seeking has been here all along, just waiting for us to notice?

One powerful way to reconnect with that happiness is through gratitude. This simple act can lift your mood, reduce stress and improve your sleep. Did you know it can also benefit your heart? By focusing on the positives in your life, you can lower blood pressure, reduce heart disease risk and strengthen your immune system. People who practise gratitude often feel fewer physical issues, like headaches or stomachaches. This thankful mindset can even add years to your life. Your perspective is your power—wield it wisely. So, take a moment to appreciate the good things and unlock the happiness waiting for us.

Rooted in thankfulness

Gratitude and the root chakra are closely connected, forming the foundation of your well-being. Practising gratitude strengthens your root chakra, helping you feel safe, secure and grounded, which empowers you to face life's challenges with confidence. A balanced root chakra allows you to appreciate the abundance in your life, no matter how small, creating a positive feedback loop that reinforces your feelings of safety and connection to the earth. Ultimately, gratitude nurtures your root chakra and anchors you to your life's purpose, fostering resilience and a deeper sense of belonging in the world.

However, without gratitude, this chakra can become blocked, leading to feelings of anxiety and fear. By embracing gratitude, you nourish your root chakra and allow positive energy to flow.

Worksheet 8: Gratitude with the root chakra worksheet for grounding your spirit

Write down, "Today, I honour the challenges I have overcome and the lessons they have brought. I am grateful for the abundance in my life and the present moment. With each breath, I reclaim my strength, find peace and release pain as a gift to myself. I embrace a life of light, wholeness and freedom, grounding my spirit in gratitude."

Affirmations for gratitude to ground your heart

- "I embrace self-compassion and find safety within my being."
- "I release negativity and anchor myself in a state of peace."
- "I cultivate security and release the past with grace."

Exercise 8.1: Start with awareness gratitude walk

This seven-day journey is about gratitude, guiding you to recognize the small, often overlooked blessings in your life. Today, start by grounding yourself in nature. Step outside, take off your shoes and feel the earth beneath your feet. As you breathe deeply, focus on the warmth of the sun, the beauty of the sky and allow gratitude to fill your heart. Awareness is the first step to gratitude—take a moment to notice simple things like a kind word or the comfort of home. Let your appreciation flow into the earth, nourishing the soil beneath you. If any negative emotions arise, gently release them, imagining them sinking into the ground, where they can be transformed. Take a piece of paper and write down what you are grateful for today—whether it is people, moments or even yourself. Bury the paper in the earth and reflect on how this practice makes you feel, remembering that you deserve this healing.

Gratitude and beej mantra meditation for the root chakra

The mantra "Lam" is vital for connecting with your root chakra. When combined with grounding techniques, it becomes a powerful tool to foster safety and emotional strength. By healing your root chakra, you open yourself to gratitude and release emotional burdens. Remember, you have the power to guide your healing journey, and each step brings you closer to a life of peace and gratitude.

- Let us begin a grounding meditation that will help you cultivate gratitude and connect with your root chakra. Start by finding a comfortable seated position, whether in a lotus

- pose or on a chair. Make sure your feet are firmly planted on the ground, and let your palms rest gently on your knees.

- Close your eyes and take a few deep breaths. Set the intention to embrace gratitude and let go of any emotional pain that weighs you down. Visualize strong roots growing from your spine, reaching deep into the earth, connecting you to its core.

- Inhale deeply and exhale while gently chanting "Lam". Imagine vibrant red energy radiating from your root chakra, dissolving any fear, insecurity and emotional turmoil. Continue chanting for 5–10 minutes, feeling that energy grounding and empowering you with each breath.

- Now, visualize three things in your life that you are truly grateful for. As you focus on each one, feel a warm wave of gratitude spreading from your heart throughout your entire body, anchoring you in the present moment. Envision these blessings surrounded by a soft, red light. As you think of each blessing, affirm, "I am grateful for this gift in my life." Repeat this a few times, allowing gratitude to fill your being.

- Slowly bring your awareness back to your breath. Open your eyes when you feel ready, and take a moment to express gratitude to Mother Earth, saying, "Thank you for supporting me and grounding me in this moment."

- Reflect on your experience. How do you feel now? Allow the calming effects of this meditation to settle within you.

Yoga for the root chakra: Nurturing gratitude from within

To further enhance this practice, start your day with light yoga. This will help you release tension and activate your root chakra, bringing you closer to a state of peace and gratitude.

Asana 8.1: Tree Pose (Vriksasana)

Stand tall and shift your weight to one foot. Place the sole of the opposite foot on your inner thigh or calf. Raise your arms overhead. This pose enhances balance and connection to the earth. Focus on your breath and appreciate the stability within you.

Asana 8.2: Seated Forward Bend (Paschimottanasana)

Sit with your legs extended in front of you. Inhale, reaching your arms up, and exhale as you fold forward, reaching for your feet. This pose promotes relaxation and grounding. Feel gratitude for the journey of self-discovery as you stretch.

Food for the root chakra

"Gratitude is the wine for the soul. Go on. Get drunk."
—Rumi

Today, focus on nourishing your root chakra with options that promote stability and gratitude. Incorporate sweet potatoes for their grounding energy, oranges to ignite creativity and joy, and nuts for healthy fats that support emotional balance. Add red foods like beets and strawberries, which symbolize vitality and strength, further enhancing your emotional well-being.

Together, these delicious choices create a nourishing and uplifting meal that encourages the free flow of feelings. Enjoy these foods as you nurture yourself on your healing journey.

Exercise 8.2: The countdown

"You ought to be thankful a whole heaping lot, for the places and people you're lucky you're not!"—Dr Seuss

The gratitude countdown is an enjoyable activity that encourages you to quickly list 10 things, people or situations you appreciate in your life, expressing gratitude for something unique with each number. This exercise is particularly useful when you are feeling low or stuck in negativity, as it can boost your mood and help you gain a more positive perspective.

To maximize your countdown, pay attention to the details. Instead of simply saying "my car" or "my home" explain what makes them special. For instance, you might say, "I'm grateful for my job because it allows me to pursue my passion and support my family" or "I appreciate my friend for always being there to listen and offer encouragement." By being specific, you create a vivid memory that genuinely evokes feelings of gratitude.

Closing Ritual: Reflect on gratitude and healing

As you conclude Day 8, find a quiet space to sit comfortably and reflect on your experiences.

What are three things you are most grateful for today?

A promise to myself

Date:

Today, as I reflect on the steps I have taken towards embracing gratitude and healing, I feel ...

………………………………………………………………………………………………………

………………………………………………………………………………………………………

………………………………………………………………………………………………………

………………………………………………………………………………………………………

………………………………………………………………………………………………………

………………………………………………………………………………………………………

………………………………………………………………………………………………………

………………………………………………………………………………………………………

I am grateful for all that I have; I am safe and secure.

Remember, this journey is deeply personal to you. Take the time you need to heal, grow and fully experience the transformative power of gratitude. As you connect with your root chakra, honour the strength and stability within you. Know that you are deserving of love, compassion and a solid foundation. Embrace the process of restoring your sense of security and grounding, and allow gratitude to guide you towards true balance and peace.

Day 9 : Gratitude—the path to deeper connections

"Gratitude is when memory is stored in the heart and not in the mind." —Lionel Hampton

Gratitude has a wonderful power to strengthen our relationships. When you show appreciation, you create deeper connections and build a sense of community. You start noticing the little joys in life—like the smiles and laughter that brighten your days.

Let me share a story about my friend Ravi. He had a loving family and a successful career, but he often felt something was missing. His focus on being perfect son, husband and father made him overlook the simple pleasures around him.

I suggested that he write down three things he was thankful for each night, no matter how small they seemed. At first, he wasn't sure it would make a difference. But soon, he began to appreciate moments like his daughter's laughter and a warm cup of tea.

As Ravi's mindset shifted, he became more patient and present with his family. The little annoyances that used to bother him faded away, and the arguments decreased. Gratitude opened his eyes to the richness of his life, allowing him to connect more deeply with the people around him. That is the magic of gratitude. When you focus on what you appreciate, you become more present and compassionate. Just embrace gratitude and experience its amazing power in your life.

Nurture bonds that matter

Gratitude and the sacral chakra are closely linked. When you practise gratitude, you open your heart to joy and creativity. This positive energy flows through your sacral chakra, enhancing your emotional well-being and relationships.

Without gratitude, you may feel disconnected or blocked. Negative emotions can build up, leading to feelings of insecurity and imbalance. But when you embrace gratitude, you release those heavy feelings, allowing your sacral chakra to thrive. This practice helps you connect deeply with yourself and others, bringing a sense of peace and joy into your life.

Worksheet 9: Gratitude with the sacral chakra worksheet for unlocking your creative flow

Write down, "Today, I embrace my emotions with openness, releasing guilt and hurt to make space for new energy. Through gratitude, I reconnect with my inner strength and creativity. I plant seeds of appreciation, trusting they will grow into joy and fulfilment. This release nurtures my growth, allowing me to feel light, inspired and free."

Affirmations for gratitude to brighten your day

- "I am thankful for my creativity, letting my emotions flow freely."
- "I invite joy and abundance, nurturing myself with gratitude."
- "With each breath, I welcome positivity and joy into my life."

Exercise 9.1: Establish creative connection with water ritual

On Day 8, you grounded yourself, feeling grateful for the stability that supports you. Now, go deeper by focusing on your creativity and emotional richness. Hold a glass of water, set a positive intention, such as "I am open to joy and creativity" or "I welcome love and support into my life",—and reflect on the relationships that nurture you and the moments that inspire you. Appreciate the joy, excitement and even the challenges that have shaped you. Feel grateful for your ability to connect and feel deeply. Slowly drink the water or splash it on your face, letting gratitude fill you. Water aligns with the sacral chakra, the heart of creativity and emotion, releasing what holds you back and inviting joy. Notice the calm that follows, a lightness in your spirit. Let this become a daily ritual—each sip or a splash of water is a reminder to be grateful. Trust that with every step, you are nourishing your spirit, growing and connecting more deeply with the life you are meant to live. Keep moving forward, day by day.

Gratitude and beej mantra meditation for the sacral chakra

Welcome to this inner child meditation designed to cultivate gratitude while nurturing your sacral chakra, located just below your navel. This chakra is essential for creativity, emotional well-being and connecting with joy. By embracing your inner child, you celebrate love and foster gratitude.

- Find a quiet, comfortable spot where you can sit undisturbed. Make the space inviting with soft lighting or calming scents. Close your eyes and take a deep breath in through your nose, allowing your belly to rise. Hold for a moment, then exhale slowly through your mouth, releasing tension. Repeat this a few times until you feel centered.

- Now, focus on your sacral chakra. Visualize a warm, vibrant orange light glowing in this area. Inhale deeply, imagining this light expanding; with each exhale, let go of heaviness, allowing gratitude to flow freely.

- Chant "Vam" on your exhale, feeling the sound resonate within you, opening the flow of creative energy. Continue this practice for several breaths, enhancing your connection to gratitude and joy.

- Visualize your younger self—full of innocence and joy. Spend a few moments with this child, soaking in their light and laughter. Express gratitude for their presence by saying, "Thank you for being you. I appreciate your joy and creativity." Allow this gratitude to wash over you.

- Repeat the affirmation: "I celebrate my inner child with gratitude and love. I embrace joy and creativity in my life."

- Slowly bring your awareness back to your breath. Open your eyes when ready and take a moment to notice how you feel. Before concluding, express gratitude for this time dedicated to yourself. Reflect on your experience and consider journaling any insights or emotions that arose. This reflection deepens your connection to gratitude and enhances your well-being.

Yoga for the sacral chakra: Nurturing gratitude from within

Start your day with some light yoga to release tension and stimulate the sacral chakra.

Asana 9.1: Low Lunge (Anjaneyasana)

By stretching the hip flexors and the lower back, this pose enhances sacral chakra energy, fostering a sense of freedom, gratitude and connection to creativity.

Asana 9.2: Cat-Cow Pose (Marjaryasana-Bitilasana)

This asana combines two movements: arching the spine upwards (Cat) and dropping the belly while lifting the chest (Cow). This gentle flow warms the spine, stretches the back and opens the hips, helping release stored emotions and fostering a natural flow of gratitude and creativity.

Food for the sacral chakra

Tropical fruits like mango and papaya are juicy and nutrient-rich, enhancing pleasure and connection to the sacral chakra. Root vegetables like sweet potatoes and carrots ground and nourish, providing stability and energy that benefit emotional balance. As you eat, imagine a warm yellow light radiating from your solar plexus chakra, filling you with gratitude for the nourishment and energy these foods bring, and allowing yourself to feel uplifted and grounded with each bite.

Exercise 9.2: Healing through art

Close your eyes, take a deep breath and let yourself relax. Now, open your eyes and start a simple drawing or painting that reflects what you are grateful for—just go with the flow without holding back. Use colours and shapes that feel joyful or warm—no need for perfection. When you are finished, look at your art and notice the gratitude it represents. This small practice brings peace and appreciation into your day.

What feelings of gratitude surfaced in your art?

………

………

Closing ritual: Reflect on gratitude and healing

As you conclude Day 9, find a quiet space to sit comfortably and reflect on your experiences.

What are the three things you are most grateful for today?

… … … …, …

… …

A promise to myself

Date:

Today, I took a meaningful step towards gratitude and renewal. I feel …

… …

… …

… …

… …

… …

… …

… …

… …

… …

I embrace the abundance in my life and welcome joy and creativity.

Remember, gratitude and creativity flow together, allowing you to connect deeply with your inner self and the world around you. By embracing your emotions with an open heart, you create space for healing and growth. Let go of past hurts and guilt, making room for vibrant energy to fill your life. Through gratitude, you unlock your creative power, nurturing joy, fulfilment and emotional well-being.

Day 10 : Gratitude—the journey to joy

> "When you focus on the good, the good gets better."
> —Abraham Hicks

Imagine waking up each morning with a heart overflowing with gratitude. Doesn't that sound wonderful? When you bring gratitude into your life, it is like stepping into a world filled with lightness and joy. Noticing the simple blessings—a flower blooming, a loved one's smile or even your own small wins—opens your eyes to beauty everywhere. This habit lifts your mood, deepens your connections and fills you with a calm sense of contentment. You will find yourself happier, more at ease and less bothered by frustrations or envy. Studies show that practising gratitude boosts your self-esteem and confidence, helping you feel amazing about yourself and others.

Science even shows us why this happens. When stress hits, your brain releases cortisol, which is what fuels those feelings of anxiety. But focusing on gratitude gently lowers cortisol and brings in a boost of natural, feel-good chemicals like serotonin and dopamine. Serotonin brings you calm and balances your mood, while dopamine gives you a sense of joy, making each moment feel worth celebrating. Gratitude isn't just a habit—it is a gentle way to bring more happiness, health and peace into your life.

Ignite inner strength

Have you ever felt that cosy, warm glow inside—a real sense of peace? That is your solar plexus chakra, the heart of your personal power, lighting up. And gratitude is the fuel that keeps it shining strong. When you feel grateful, your inner light grows. You feel capable, grounded and full of confidence. But without gratitude, that light fades, leaving room for doubt and insecurity. You might even feel disconnected from your own strength.

The good news? You can nurture your inner power by practising gratitude. Let your heart fill with thankfulness and watch your confidence bloom. Take a moment to appreciate your journey—it strengthens the light within you.

Worksheet 10: Gratitude with the solar plexus chakra worksheet for illuminating your inner power

Write down, "Today, I embrace gratitude and release what no longer serves me. With each breath, I plant a seed of thankfulness, allowing it to grow into peace and confidence. This release empowers me to move forward, unburdened and filled with appreciation, strengthening my inner power and supporting my personal growth."

Affirmations for gratitude and inner power

- "I am thankful for my inner light and the confidence it brings."

- "I welcome joy and abundance, strengthening my self-worth."

- "With each breath, I embrace growth and celebrate my journey."

Exercise 10.1: Personal triumphs and the gratitude jar

This seven-day gratitude journey invites you to celebrate every part of your life. Day 8 was about honouring stability, and Day 9 focused on creativity and emotional richness. Today, on Day 10, take a moment to acknowledge your strengths and achievements. Create a gratitude jar and, each day, write down something you are thankful for—a joyful memory, a kind word or a personal success. Today, appreciate the talents that have brought you to where you are and take pride in every accomplishment, no matter how small. At the end of the week or month, revisit your notes and cherish the uplifting moments. Share the practice with your family by decorating the jar together, adding themes or making it a fun tradition. This simple habit goes beyond just counting blessings; it nurtures joy and strengthens connections. Keep this ritual going throughout your 21-day journey and beyond, allowing it to fill your days with gratitude and warmth, one small note at a time.

Gratitude and beej mantra meditation for the solar plexus chakra

"Ram" is the mantra for the solar plexus chakra, and when you use this mantra during your meditation, you tap into a powerful source of gratitude and self-empowerment. The Ram mantra energizes your solar plexus, filling you with courage and a deep appreciation for your unique self. Together, they open the door to embracing your authentic being.

- Find a peaceful spot where you can sit comfortably. Take a deep breath in, inviting in positive energy and exhale any heaviness or negativity that you have been carrying.

- Inhale deeply, and as you exhale, chant "Ram". Visualize a warm, golden light radiating from your solar plexus chakra, just above your navel. This light helps dissolve feelings of doubt and fear, filling you with confidence and gratitude. With each breath, feel this energy growing brighter and stronger, wrapping you in warmth and love. If emotions come up, welcome them as essential parts of your healing journey.

- Imagine a warm light in your solar plexus, lifting away everything that holds you back. With each deep breath, think about something you are thankful for in your life. This light symbolizes your growth, turning past struggles into lessons. Let this warmth fill you with energy, helping you take steps towards your dreams. When you embrace gratitude, it brightens your spirit and encourages you to share your true self with the world.

- Now, repeat this affirmation: "I embrace gratitude and acknowledge my strength. I am worthy of joy and success." Say it out loud or write it down to strengthen its presence in your life.

- Gradually bring your focus back to your breath. When you are ready, gently open your eyes and express gratitude for this healing moment, saying, "Thank you for helping me recognize my power."

- Allow the effects of your practice to settle in, and consider jotting down any thoughts or feelings that emerged during your meditation. This reflection deepens your understanding and supports your ongoing journey of gratitude and empowerment.

Yoga for the solar plexus chakra: Nurturing gratitude from within

Begin your day with gentle yoga to release tension and energize your solar plexus chakra. Embrace these poses to cultivate appreciation and empower your spirit as you move through your day.

Asana 10.1: Bow Pose (Dhanurasana)

This pose opens your heart and strengthens your core, enhancing your sense of gratitude and personal power.

Asana 10.2: High Lunge Twist with Anjali Mudra (Prayer Position)

This dynamic stretch encourages grounding and reflection, allowing you to express gratitude while fostering a deeper connection to yourself.

Food for the solar plexus chakra

Foods that nourish and empower the solar plexus chakra (manipura) include bananas, pineapples, turmeric and mangoes. These foods boost your energy and help balance this chakra, which is linked to personal power and confidence. Incorporating gratitude into your daily life amplifies your connection to this chakra, promoting positive emotions and self-acceptance. By savouring these foods and practising gratitude, you create a strong foundation for your self-worth and inner strength.

Exercise 10.2: Reflect and celebrate your blessings

Take a piece of paper and set an alarm for 10 minutes. Write down all the things, people and experiences you are grateful for. Be honest and thorough. Once the time is up, read through your list and reflect on how these blessings have impacted your life.

....

....

....

....

....

....

....

....

....

How do you feel now that you have acknowledged your gratitude?

....

... ...

... ...

... ...

... ...

... ...

... ...

... ...

... ...

What is something you often take for granted?

... ...

... ...

... ...

... ...

... ...

... ...

... ...

....

....

Closing Ritual: Reflect on gratitude and healing

As you conclude Day 10, find a quiet space to sit comfortably and reflect on your experiences.

What are the three things you are most grateful for today?

....

....

....

....

....

....

....

....

A promise to myself

Date:

Today, I embraced the power of gratitude and took a meaningful step towards self-empowerment. I feel ...

I embrace my inner strength and celebrate the abundance in my life.

Gratitude isn't just a mental health trick; it is a way to improve your life. It fuels your inner strength and lights your path to happiness. When you begin your day with a grateful heart, you create more peace and balance in your life.

Day 11 : Gratitude—the glue that binds hearts

"The heart that gives thanks is a happy one, for we cannot feel thankful and unhappy at the same time."—Douglas Wood

Have you ever felt the warmth of a truly loving connection? It is a beautiful feeling, isn't it? Well, imagine making those connections even stronger, filling your life with more joy and happiness. You can do that by practising gratitude. It is not just good for your heart and mind, but it also strengthens your relationships in incredible ways. When you express your thanks, it shows others you truly value them, fostering a sense of belonging and making your bonds stronger.

Thus, expressing gratitude can make your relationships even better, creating more trust and happiness. When you appreciate your loved ones, you build a foundation of positivity and support, making it easier to overcome challenges together. It is like the glue that keeps everything strong, promoting open communication and deeper love.

Gratitude is a personal journey, unique to you. When you share your thankfulness, you strengthen your connections with others. It is like a warm hug for both your soul and theirs. Start small—write in a gratitude journal, practise mindfulness or simply notice the beauty around you. You will be surprised at how this tiny shift can bring immense peace and fulfilment in to your life. Remember, it are the small things that often have the biggest impact.

Your heart blossoms with gratitude

Have you ever felt that deep ache in your chest, a longing for connection? That is your heart chakra, and it yearns for love and appreciation. When you are grateful, your heart chakra blossoms. It opens wide, allowing love to flow freely, both to you and from you. It is like your own personal fountain of joy and connection. But without gratitude, it closes, like a flower in the dark. You might feel disconnected, lonely and even resentful. Imagine your heart filled with sunshine and warmth—that is what gratitude can do for your heart chakra and your life. Choose gratitude and let your heart sing its sweetest song.

Worksheet 11: Beej mantra meditation to awaken your inner light

Write down, "Today, I embrace gratitude as a part of my journey to self-discovery. I release anything that dims my heart's light, creating space for love and joy to enter. With each breath, I feel warmth and appreciation growing within, filling my heart. My heart chakra opens, allowing love to flow both inwards and outwards. This feeling nurtures me, a reminder that gratitude leads me forward with peace, love and connection."

Affirmations for gratitude and compassion

- "I welcome love with an open heart."
- "I give and receive love with gratitude."
- "Each breath fills my heart with healing and peace."

Exercise 11.1: Love, compassion and acts of kindness

"The best way to find yourself is to lose yourself in the service of others."—Mahatma Gandhi

The journey so far has already helped you reflect on stability, creativity and your personal strengths. Now, let us turn to love and compassion. Think of all the love and kindness you have received—those little acts of care that have lifted your spirits. Now, think of the love you have to give. Because kindness is the language which the deaf can hear and the blind can see. And doesn't even cost you anything. Take a moment to be thankful for your ability to show kindness, whether it is through a smile, a helping hand or just listening to someone who needs support. Today, I invite you to practise small acts of kindness.

Hold the door open for someone, offer a compliment or help someone with a task. Notice how good it feels to spread kindness and how it fills your heart with warmth. Reflect on the impact these small gestures have, both on others and on you. Keep a journal of your acts of kindness and how they make you feel. Remember, kindness creates a ripple effect, and every small act brings more love into the world, starting with you. This gratitude journey isn't just about receiving; it is about giving and connecting.

Gratitude and beej mantra meditation for the heart chakra

The mantra "Yam" is linked to the heart chakra, making it a wonderful tool for cultivating gratitude. By focusing on this mantra during meditation, you create a space for love and appreciation to flow freely, healing emotional wounds and nurturing connections with yourself and others.

- To begin, find a quiet spot where you can sit comfortably. Close your eyes and take several deep breaths to ground yourself. Start by gently chanting or repeating the mantra "Yam". Visualize your heart chakra at the centre of your chest. With each repetition of "Yam", imagine a warm, green light expanding from your heart, filling your body with love and gratitude. Let this light melt away any tension or negativity, creating space for joy and appreciation. Continue this for about 2–3 minutes.

- Focus on four phrases that embody gratitude and love. Say or think each of the following phrases softly:

  » "I appreciate you": Acknowledge the positive impact this person has had in your life.

> » "I am grateful for the lessons": Reflect on the growth gained from your experiences together.
>
> » "Thank you for being in my life": Express gratitude for their presence and support.
>
> » "I love you": Open your heart wide, sending love and warmth to this person.

As you say these phrases, visualize someone special in front of you, feeling the warmth and sincerity behind each word.

- After repeating these phrases, return your attention to your breath. Feel the peace that comes from expressing gratitude and letting go of anything weighing you down. When you are ready, slowly open your eyes and express gratitude by saying, "Thank you for helping me connect with my heart."

- Finally, reflect on your feelings. Consider writing down any insights or emotions that surfaced during your meditation, allowing this practice to deepen your sense of gratitude and strengthen your heart chakra.

Yoga for the heart chakra: Nurturing gratitude from within

Begin your day with gentle yoga to cultivate gratitude and awaken your heart chakra.

Asana 11.1: Warrior Seal (Virabhadra Mudra)

This gesture cultivates a sense of gratitude and helps align your energy with the heart chakra. As you practise this mudra, focus on feelings of appreciation for the people and experiences in your life.

Asana 11.2: Prayer Squat (Namaskarasana)

This pose promotes a deep connection to the earth while fostering a sense of groundedness and openness in your heart space. As you settle into the squat, embrace the stability beneath you, inviting love and gratitude to flow freely within you.

Food for the heart chakra

Nourish your heart chakra and uplift your spirit with foods that encourage gratitude. Include foods like parsley, celery, cucumbers, zucchini, matcha, green tea, avocados, limes, mint, peas, kiwis, spirulina and green apples in your diet. These choices help balance your heart chakra, inviting love and appreciation into your life.

Leafy greens and wholesome fruits foster emotional healing, while foods like avocados, rich in healthy fats, promote self-love and resilience. Together, these nourishing ingredients work to open your heart, allowing you to release negativity and embrace gratitude. Let each meal remind you of life's beauty, enriching your journey towards love and inner peace.

Swadhyaya (self-reflection)

To practice gratitude and reflect on your heart chakra, try the swadhyaya (self-reflection) exercise. This exercise helps you gain perspective on your relationships and fosters appreciation by promoting empathy and understanding. It is a way to open your heart and deepen your connections with others, leading to greater compassion for yourself and others. Reflect on these three questions, focusing on a specific person, relationship or event:

What have you received from this person? Consider the support, love or lessons they have provided you.

....

....

....

....

What have you given to this person? Think about the help, love or time you have shared with them.

....

....

....

....

....

....

....

....

What troubles or difficulties have you caused this person? Acknowledge any hurtful actions or words that may have affected them.

....

....

....

....

....

....

....

....

....

....

Take a moment to reflect on these answers and express gratitude for the lessons learned and the relationships you have. This practice is not just about forgiveness but about cultivating love and understanding within yourself and nurturing your connections with others. By connecting with the heart chakra, you open yourself to emotional healing and greater peace.

Closing ritual: Reflect on gratitude and healing

As you conclude Day 11, find a quiet space to sit comfortably and reflect on your experiences.

What are three things you are most grateful for today?

....

....

....

....

………………………………………………………………………………………

………………………………………………………………………………………

………………………………………………………………………………………

………………………………………………………………………………………

………………………………………………………………

A promise to myself

Date:

Today, as I reflect on the steps I have taken towards embracing gratitude and healing, I feel …

………………………………………………………………………………………

………………………………………………………………………………………

………………………………………………………………………………………

………………………………………………………………………………………

………………………………………………………………………………………

………………………………………………………………………………………

………………………………………………………………………………………

I am grateful for the love and kindness that surrounds me.

When you embrace gratitude, your heart opens, inviting deeper compassion and understanding towards others. This warmth creates more meaningful connections and strengthens the support network around you, filling your life with positivity and love.

Day 12 : Gratitude—awaken the voice within

"Not what we have, but what we enjoy, constitutes our happiness."—Epicurus

Gratitude is not always easy, especially on hard days when life feels heavy, and finding something to appreciate seems impossible. But those are the moments when gratitude is most powerful—and truly worth it.

On days like these, start small. Don't push yourself to find big things; instead, appreciate the basics. Be grateful for simply being here, for the food you have, for a place to rest, or the presence of someone who cares. Even in the hardest times, there is always something to hold on to, no matter how small. Over time, these little moments of gratitude can fill your heart, gently shifting your perspective.

As you make gratitude a habit, you will notice a lightness in your life. Challenges become more manageable, your relationships deepen and you will feel stronger within.

So, take a moment to pause and ask yourself, *What am I thankful for today?* Notice the tiny, beautiful moments you may have missed. Let your heart fill with appreciation and feel how it changes your outlook. Start today, simply by asking yourself, *What am I grateful for?* You will be amazed at how much it transforms you.

Open up through gratitude

Have you ever felt a lump in your throat, a tightness that holds you back from speaking your truth? That is your throat chakra, the centre of self-expression. When you embrace gratitude, this chakra opens, letting your voice flow clear and true. Gratitude allows your words to become like a beautiful song—you can speak your mind without fear, and it feels liberating. Without it, your throat chakra can close, leaving you hesitant and silent. Imagine expressing your love, passion and truth freely every day. Let gratitude be your guide, opening your heart and voice. Let your words flow with love and thankfulness. You are worthy of full expression; your voice deserves to be heard.

Worksheet 12: Gratitude with throat chakra worksheet for embracing authentic expression

Write down, "Today, I embrace gratitude and let it flow through my words. I focus on the simple joys around me, allowing appreciation to fill my heart and open my throat chakra. I honour my feelings and speak my truth with confidence and love. As I express gratitude, I invite clarity into my voice, strengthening my connection with myself and others. Today is a celebration of my true voice and the power of gratitude.

Affirmations for gratitude and clear expression

- "I express gratitude freely, allowing my words to flow with ease."

- "I speak with kindness, embracing my true voice."
- "Each breath fills me with peace and joy, empowering my expression."

Exercise 12.1: Express gratitude and communicate appreciation

As you continue this seven-day gratitude journey, building on the stability, creativity, strength and love you have already embraced, today, on Day 12, it is time to express appreciation. Think of someone who has made a difference in your life. Reach out and tell them exactly why they matter to you. Share a specific memory or a moment when their kindness touched you. Let them know the qualities you admire and encourage them to keep shining.

This is also an opportunity to activate your throat chakra. Reflect on the times you have communicated honestly and been heard. Speaking your truth is powerful, and expressing gratitude strengthens your relationships.

Take a moment to reflect on how expressing gratitude made you feel. Gratitude is not just about what you feel; it is about what you give. Make it a habit—thank someone new each week. Watch how your words create deeper connections and spread positivity and love.

Gratitude and beej mantra meditation for the throat chakra

This meditation invites you to reconnect with your authentic voice while nurturing a deep sense of gratitude. By focusing on the beej mantra "Ham", you can balance your throat chakra, creating space for clear and peaceful self-expression. Let gratitude flow through you, opening your throat chakra to welcome your true self.

- Begin by finding a serene space to sit comfortably. With your back straight, close your eyes and rest your hands on your lap. Take several deep breaths, allowing your body and mind to unwind.

- As you inhale deeply, softly exhale while chanting "Ham". Whisper it or say it aloud—whichever feels natural. Visualize a soothing blue light in your throat, expansive and calm like a clear sky. With each breath, let this light grow stronger, opening your throat chakra and allowing your true feelings to flow freely.

- Continue breathing into this light, letting it shine brighter with every exhale. Feel the comforting vibrations wrap around you, bringing warmth and peace. If emotions arise, embrace them; they are part of your healing journey.

- Now, connect with your intention for this meditation. Perhaps you want to cultivate gratitude for the present moment, appreciate your journey, or recognize the beauty around you. Hold this intention close as you breathe, grounding yourself in this purpose. Remind yourself: "I am grateful for my true self and open to all that uplifts me." Writing this affirmation can deepen its significance.

- Spend a few moments in stillness, allowing the meditation's energy to settle within you. Embrace the calm and clarity that fill your heart.

When you feel ready, take a deep breath and bring your awareness back to the present. Notice any lightness or peace within you, and carry this sense of healing forward. Remember, you have the strength to heal, and every step brings you closer to your true self. Trust your journey and embrace the path ahead.

Yoga for the throat chakra: Nurturing gratitude from within

Begin your day with a gentle yoga practice designed to foster gratitude and enhance the flow of energy through your throat chakra. This mindful approach helps to release any tension and creates space for your authentic voice to emerge.

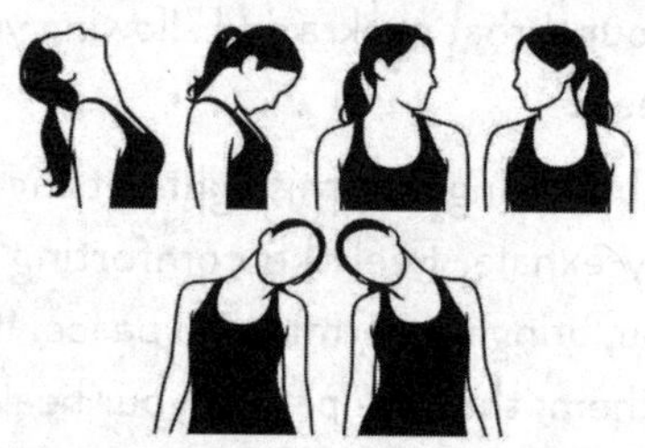

Asana 12.1: Neck Rolls (Greeva Sanchalanasana)

This simple yet effective movement helps to relieve stiffness and promote relaxation in the neck area. As you roll your neck, visualize tension melting away, allowing gratitude to flow freely through your throat.

Asana 12.2: Halasana (Plow Pose)

This pose not only stretches the throat and shoulders but also calms the nervous system, helping to cultivate a deeper sense of appreciation for your body and voice.

Food for the throat chakra

Nourish your throat chakra with mindful eating that celebrates healing and gratitude. Enjoy each bite of nutrient-rich foods, allowing their flavours to enhance your connection to your true self. Focus on vibrant options like blueberries, blackberries and warm herbal teas, which not only taste delightful but also support emotional balance and clear expression.

Take the time to appreciate the textures and tastes, and reflect on the nourishment they bring to your body and spirit. By savouring these healing bites, you create a deeper sense of gratitude for the gifts of nature, empowering your voice and inviting love and compassion into your life.

Exercise 12.2: No whining day

"Learn to be thankful for what you already have, while you pursue all that you want."—Jim Rohn

Challenge yourself to go an entire day without complaining. Committing to a No Whining Day can transform your outlook on life. Research shows that constant complaining lowers happiness, but focusing on positivity can shift your mindset. Set the intention to stay complaint-free and pay attention to your thoughts. If you feel the urge to complain, pause and breathe, replace those thoughts with gratitude for the little things.

If you slip up, be kind to yourself—it is part of the journey. Notice how this shift changes your mood and energy, and with practice, increasing your complaint-free days will become easier. Reflect on your day.

What moments made you want to complain, and how did shifting to gratitude change your mood or interactions?

... ...

... ...

... ...

... ...

... ...

... ...

... ...

... ...

What did I learn about my mindset?

... ...

... ...

... ...

....

....

....

....

....

....

How can I practise more gratitude in my life?

....

....

....

....

....

....

....

....

....

Closing ritual: Reflect on gratitude and healing

As you conclude Day 12, find a quiet space to sit comfortably and reflect on your experiences.

What are the three things you are most grateful for today?

....

....

....

....

....

....

....

....

....

A promise to myself

Date:

Today, I embraced the power of gratitude and took a meaningful step towards self-empowerment. I feel ...

....

....

....

....

....

....

....

....

....

....

I express gratitude clearly and with love, welcoming peace into my life.

True healing begins with choosing to speak your truth and releasing what no longer supports you. Embrace this path with gratitude, allowing your throat chakra to open and guide you towards growth, clarity and inner peace.

Day 13 : Gratitude—find calm amid the chaos

"There is a calmness to a life lived in gratitude, a quiet joy."
—Ralph H. Blum

Have you ever wished there was an easy way to feel calmer, sharper and more at ease? Imagine waking up refreshed, your mind clear, ready to face the day with energy. It is possible, and it all starts with practising a small habit: gratitude.

Practising gratitude helps shift your focus toward the positive aspects of life. It encourages your mind to let go of worry and stress, helping you feel more balanced and peaceful. This gentle change can support better sleep, reduce anxiety and help you handle life's challenges with greater ease.

Isn't it incredible that something so small can have such a big impact on your life? Start today—pause, breathe and think of something you are grateful for. Just a few moments of appreciation can brighten your days and lighten your load. Let gratitude be your guide, and watch as it transforms your days into something brighter, calmer and more joyful. You deserve it.

Open the door to intuition

"Intuition is the whisper of the soul." – Jiddu Krishnamurti

Have you ever felt that deep sense of wonder, that feeling of being part of something bigger? That is your third eye chakra awakening—the gateway to intuition, wisdom and inner knowing. When you practise gratitude, you open that door a bit wider. Feeling thankful brings light to the beauty and blessings around you, letting your third eye shine brighter and revealing your inner guidance.

Gratitude is more than just noticing the good; it gently opens your mind, easing worries and bringing clarity. Each grateful thought clears a path for your third eye, inviting insight and peace.

Worksheet 13: Gratitude with the third eye chakra worksheet for awakening clarity and insight

Write down, "Today, I embrace gratitude, honouring the lessons I have learned. I let go of past worries and trust my intuition to lead me. With each breath, clarity grows, revealing the beauty inside and around me. I deserve this peace and the freedom to be present.

I nurture my inner wisdom, planting a seed of light that will guide and illuminate my path each day."

Affirmations for gratitude and inner clarity

- "I am grateful for the clarity and guidance I receive."
- "I trust my inner wisdom and welcome gratitude into my life."
- "With each breath, I release negativity and embrace peace and insight."

Exercise 13.1: Insight, intuition and the empty chair exercise

On Day 13, deepen your practice with visualization and communication. Take a quiet moment to close your eyes and picture the things you are grateful for: the people, experiences and blessings in your life. Feel the emotions that come with this gratitude—joy, love, peace.

Find a space where you can set up two chairs. One is for you, the other for someone you want to thank. Sit on one chair and speak directly to the empty chair, sharing how they have positively impacted your life. Switch chairs and imagine their response, considering how your gratitude makes them feel. Focus on your third eye chakra, visualizing an indigo light that sharpens your intuition and enhances your clarity. Reflect on your emotions, and ask yourself what insights came up. This practice not only deepens your connection to others, but also nurtures your sense of gratitude.

Gratitude, trataka and beej mantra meditation for the third eye chakra

The mantra "Om" resonates deeply with the third eye chakra, serving as a powerful tool for enhancing intuition and insight. When practised through the ancient meditation technique *trataka* meditation, it transforms into a meaningful experience for cultivating gratitude. Trataka means "to gaze steadily" in Sanskrit. Chanting "Om" aligns and energizes your third eye, while trataka meditation sharpens your mental focus, paving the way for emotional clarity and a greater appreciation for life.

- Find a quiet and comfortable spot to sit. Light a candle and place it at eye level, about an arm's length away. This flame will be your focal point for trataka meditation. As you breathe in, invite positive energy into your being, and as you exhale, let go of tension and negativity.

- Softly gaze at the candle flame without blinking for about 2 minutes, allowing its warm glow to envelop you. Afterwards, close your eyes and hold the mental image of the flame for an additional 3 minutes, connecting with the tranquility it offers.

- Allow the flame to draw you deeper into your practice. Shift your attention to your third eye chakra, located between your eyebrows. Inhale deeply, and as you exhale, begin chanting "Om". Repeat the mantra silently or aloud for 2–3 minutes. Visualize a soothing indigo light expanding from your third eye chakra, dissolving doubt and inviting clarity. With each breath, feel this light growing brighter, resonating within you for 4–5 minutes, wrapping you in warmth and gratitude.

- After your mantra practice, repeat the affirmation: "I embrace my inner wisdom and the power of gratitude. I am worthy of clarity and joy." Speak it aloud or write it down to reinforce its significance in your heart.

- Gradually bring your focus back to your breath. When you are ready, gently open your eyes and express gratitude for this moment of clarity by saying, "Thank you for helping me see the beauty within and around me."

- Allow the effects of your meditation to settle within you. Consider jotting down any insights or feelings that emerged during your practice.

Yoga for the third eye chakra: Nurturing gratitude from within

Begin your day with a gentle yoga flow to open your third eye chakra and invite clarity, intuition and gratitude. This practice helps release mental blockages and tension, allowing your inner wisdom to emerge.

Asana 13.1: Tree Pose (Vriksasana)

Build balance and focus, connecting with your inner vision. With each breath, deepen your awareness and invite clarity to flow through your mind and body.

Asana 13.2: Dolphin Pose (Ardha Pincha Mayurasana)

Open the heart and strengthen communication. Visualize energy flowing through your third eye, enhancing intuition and bringing peaceful clarity, all the while deepening your gratitude.

Food for third chakra

Nourish your body with foods that enhance your third eye chakra and promote mental clarity, intuition and gratitude. Consider including foods like blueberries, eggplant, dark chocolate, and other purple-hued fruits and vegetables.

These vibrant foods support your inner vision and help clear your mind, allowing you to connect more deeply with your inner wisdom and express gratitude in every moment.

Exercise 13.2: Letter of gratitude

"A grateful mind is a great mind which eventually attracts to itself great things."—Plato

Writing a letter of gratitude allows you to express appreciation and deepen your connection to your third eye chakra. This practice encourages clarity by helping you acknowledge the positive influence others have had on your life. Because feeling grateful and not expressing it is like wrapping a present and not giving it.

Begin by addressing someone who has made a meaningful impact. Use "I" statements to clearly convey your gratitude, such as "I felt supported when ..." Share specific examples of how their kindness or guidance has uplifted you. As you write, consider any challenges this person may have faced, which can deepen your compassion. A moment of gratitude makes a difference in your attitude.

Reflect on how your life has changed for the better due to their presence, recognizing that expressing gratitude opens the door to healing and connection.

When you finish, create a simple ritual: read your letter aloud, as if speaking directly to them. You may choose to keep the letter as a reminder or release it by burning, symbolizing your intention to hold on to these positive feelings. Afterwards, reflect on your experience with the following questions:

What made you want to write this letter to that person? How did you feel before you began?

....

....

....

What thought patterns prevent you from expressing gratitude?

....

....

....

....

....

....

....

What steps can you take to shift these thought patters and strengthen your relationships?

....

....

....

Closing ritual: *Reflect* on gratitude and healing

As you conclude Day 13, find a quiet space to sit comfortably and reflect on your experiences.

What are the three things you are most grateful for today?

A promise to myself

Date:

Today, I took a profound step towards expressing gratitude and healing through forgiveness. I feel ...

... ...

... ...

... ...

... ...

... ...

... ...

... ...

... ...

... ...

I release the past; I open my mind to clarity and intuition.

Gratitude nurtures insight, allowing us to see beyond the surface and appreciate life's deeper gifts. Through the third eye chakra, we gain clarity and intuition, helping us connect with a profound sense of purpose and understanding.

Day 14 : Gratitude—nourish the soul

"What separates privilege from entitlement is gratitude."
—Brené Brown

Have you ever noticed that beautiful moments slip by because you are too busy thinking about what's next? I know I have, and it is a sad realization. We get so caught up chasing happiness that we forget to appreciate what is right in front of us.

I was once running my own race, always striving for that "next thing" I thought would make me happy. But one evening changed everything. After a terrible accident, I found myself at home, feeling shaken and relieved, and suddenly, it hit me—I already had so much to be grateful for. My home wasn't just a place; it was a safe haven filled with memories. The people in my life were not just familiar faces; they were my warmth and my purpose. And above all, I was alive.

Since that day, I have made a real effort to practise gratitude, and it has transformed my life. Shifting my focus from what I lack to what I have has brought me peace, patience and a deeper connection with others. It is time to stop and appreciate the beauty that surrounds you.

A journey to wisdom and unity

Have you ever felt that deep, fulfilling peace that seems to come from beyond you? That is the gift of an open crown chakra, the centre of connection and higher awareness. Gratitude is a powerful way to nourish this energy—it grounds us in appreciation and opens us to something greater than ourselves.

When we practise gratitude, we welcome a sense of unity, purpose and calm. Without it, though, the crown chakra can feel blocked, leaving us disconnected and searching. Embracing gratitude brings us closer to our inner light, creating a bridge to our highest wisdom and deepest peace.

Worksheet 14: Gratitude with the crown chakra worksheet for embracing spiritual clarity

Write down, "Today, I welcome gratitude into my heart, appreciating every step and lesson of this journey. I release past worries and trust my inner wisdom to lead me. Each breath brings clarity, revealing the beauty within me and the world. I am worthy of peace and the present moment. By nurturing my intuition and calm, I plant a seed of light, trusting it to grow and guide me gently each day."

Affirmations for gratitude and enlightenment

- "I release fear and welcome gratitude into my life."
- "I trust the wisdom within and around me, allowing peace to flow."
- "With every breath, I let go of negativity and embrace clarity."

Exercise 14.1: Embrace higher consciousness and shift your perspective

"We should certainly count our blessings, but we should also make our blessings count."—Neil A. Maxwell

As you reach Day 14 of this gratitude journey, reflect on all the blessings you have acknowledged so far—your stability, creativity, strengths, love and acts of kindness. Today, shift your focus to gratitude for your spiritual journey and the higher forces that guide you. Take a deep breath and recognize the greater power that supports you, even in the most challenging times. Think about a current challenge you are facing. Feel the emotions but don't let them define you. Find at least one thing you can be grateful for, no matter how small. Gratitude, especially in tough moments, helps you stay hopeful and resilient. Ask yourself, *What can I learn from this? What's the silver lining?* Reframe negative thoughts into positive ones. Affirm, *I choose to see the blessings in my life.* As you reflect on how gratitude shifts your perspective, carry that feeling with you. Notice how it changes your energy and the insights you gain. Gratitude truly transforms.

Gratitude, five senses and beej mantra meditation for the crown chakra

This meditation helps you ground yourself in the present moment by engaging your senses and inviting gratitude to flow freely. By focusing on your surroundings and your crown chakra, you clear stress, calm your mind and reconnect with peace. As you embrace each sensation, you open yourself to gratitude and higher awareness, lifting your spirit. Chanting a simple crown chakra mantra, like "Om", can enhance this connection, helping you create space for clarity and deeper understanding. This practice encourages presence, gratitude, and the abundance of the here and now.

- Find a quiet, comfortable space to sit, close your eyes and take a deep breath. Let go of any tension as you focus on your breath, becoming calmer and more centred. Begin silently repeating the mantra "Om", focusing on the crown chakra at the top of your head. Visualize a warm violet light radiating from this space, filling you with peace, love, compassion and understanding. Allow this light to dissolve any negativity or anger. Stay with this for a few minutes.

- Now, shift your focus to your senses. Notice three things you can see, hear, smell, taste and touch. Observe the details around you—whether it is a picture, sunlight or the texture of your surroundings. Hear the sounds, whether it is the rustling leaves or a distant chatter, and acknowledge how they enhance your moment. Pay attention to any scents in the air, savouring them. If you have something to taste, enjoy it fully and reflect on the flavours and textures. Bring awareness to the sensations of touch, whether it is the surface beneath you or the warmth of your hands. With each sense, say to yourself, *I am grateful for this moment.*

- Afterwards, take a few deep breaths, inhale deeply and exhale slowly. Gently wiggle your fingers and toes to bring awareness back to your body. Take a moment to notice how you feel and carry this sense of gratitude with you throughout your day. Let this meditation help you appreciate the present moment and the small joys that surround you.

Yoga for the crown chakra: Nurturing gratitude from within

Start with a mindful flow to awaken your crown chakra, inviting clarity, gratitude and higher wisdom.

Asana 14.1: Wide-Legged Standing Forward Bend (Prasarita Padottanasana)

Release tension and clear mental fog by grounding yourself in gratitude and openness to higher consciousness.

Asana 14.2: Standing Prayer Backbend (Anuvittasana)

Open your heart and invite the expansive energy of the crown chakra, filling you with peace and divine connection.

Food for the crown chakra

Nourish both gratitude and your crown chakra by choosing foods that bring calm and clarity. White and purple foods, like coconut, cauliflower and purple cabbage, align with the crown chakra's energy and help foster peace. These simple, nourishing foods encourage openness and invite us to release mental clutter, making room for a gentle sense of gratitude.

Coconut offers a natural soothing quality, while purple cabbage and cauliflower provide uplifting nutrients that support a clear mind and open heart. As you enjoy these mindful bites, feel yourself embracing tranquility, letting go of old stress and cultivating gratitude for the present moment.

Exercise 14.2: Write a letter of gratitude to yourself

"Sometimes it's the journey that teaches you a lot about your destination."—Drake

Find a quiet, peaceful space where you won't be disturbed. Take a piece of paper and begin writing a letter to yourself, focusing on acknowledging your strengths and expressing gratitude for the growth you have achieved. Use gentle, kind words—acknowledge what you have learned and express appreciation for your journey. Because the journey itself is the reward.

As you write, remind yourself that every experience contributes to your personal growth and you deserve to recognize your progress. Remember, the struggles along the path are meant to shape you, not break you. When you finish, read the letter back to yourself. Reflect on how it feels to acknowledge your achievements and express gratitude for your journey.

"Success is a journey, not a destination. The doing is often more important than the outcome."—Arthur Ashe

After embracing self-compassion, do you feel lighter, more at peace and happier?

How can you incorporate this gratitude practice into your routine?

Closing Ritual: Reflect on gratitude and healing

Congratulations on completing two weeks. Take a moment to reflect on the emotions you have released along the way. Notice how your heart feels lighter and more open now.

What are the three things you are most grateful for today?

… …

… …

… …

… …

… …

… …

… …

… …

… …

A promise to myself

Date:

What positive changes have you noticed in yourself and others during these two week? What specific moments or experiences have you felt particularly grateful for?

....

....

....

....

....

....

....

....

....

*I release all attachments; I open my mind to universal love
and guidance.*

Gratitude is a continuous journey. Now that you have found the path, keep moving forward to create a life filled with happiness and joy for yourself and those around you. Keep going—you are building something beautiful.

Congratulations on completing Week 2

Take a moment to truly celebrate the incredible progress you have made. Your courage in facing your emotions and committing to your healing journey is nothing short of inspiring. This path may not have been easy, but you have bravely taken the first step, and that alone is a monumental achievement. You have gifted yourself the opportunity for growth and learned to open your heart to gratitude.

As you continue forward, remember that gratitude is not just a fleeting act; it is a powerful way of life. By expressing gratitude to others, you cultivate deeper connections, and by extending that same appreciation to yourself, you embrace self-compassion. Each time you acknowledge the positive aspects of your life, you create a beautiful space for love and light to flourish.

Remember, true peace comes from within. Releasing negativity allows you to live fully, with a heart open to joy and new beginnings. You are stronger than your past, and every step you take towards gratitude propels you towards a more peaceful and fulfilled life.

Now, as you enter the final week of this journey, you have let go of the past and are living in the present. It is time to design the future of your dreams.

"The more you praise and celebrate your life, the more there is in life to celebrate." – Oprah Winfrey

What are your key takeaways from this week?

....

....

....

....

....

WEEK 3

8 Manifestation— Shape Your Future

"Destiny is not a matter of chance, it is a matter of choice."
—William Jennings Bryan

Welcome to Week 3. You have come so far already, and now it is time to step into the future you have been dreaming of. You have laid the foundation—clearing mental clutter, practising forgiveness and aligning with gratitude. Now, the magic of manifestation begins. This week, it is about shifting from the present to the future. It is time to believe, truly believe, that your goals are within reach. You have set yourself up for success, but now it is time to take action.

The journey you are on isn't about waiting for things to happen. It is about making them happen. It is about showing up every day, even in small ways, to move closer to the life you want. Because what you think, you create; what you feel, you attract; what you imagine, you become. *Every step, no matter how small, counts.* The more you commit to this process, the more your thoughts will shift, your actions will align and your dreams will feel closer.

"Every intention sets energy into motion, whether you are aware of it or not."—Gary Zukav

This week's practices only take 45 minutes to an hour, but they will help you build a habit that lasts. As you follow along, you will notice your outlook changing, your energy shifting and your belief growing stronger. These are not just exercises for now—they are tools you will carry with you far beyond these 21 days.

Remember, it is not about perfection. It is about progress. Every step forward is a victory. You have already shown yourself what is possible, so now it is time to show the universe you are ready. Trust the process, trust yourself and know that you have the power to create the life you have always wanted. Keep going—the best is yet to come.

Day 15 : Manifestation—your journey to true transformation

You have probably noticed the buzz around manifestation—on social media, in books, in conversations with friends. I was sceptical too, wondering if our thoughts could really shape our lives. But trust me, manifestation is so much more than a trend; it is a powerful practice that truly works.

Manifestation is about aligning your thoughts, beliefs and actions with your desires. It is focusing on what you want, believing in it and taking steps to bring it into reality. You are not just wishing; you are actively creating the life you dream of. It is a journey of trusting yourself, staying connected to your goals and having faith that what you seek is already on its way.

> "You manifest what you believe, not what you want."—Sonia Ricotti

Are you ready to take charge of your life and experience this transformative journey? Trust yourself and watch as your reality shifts in ways you never imagined. Your dreams are closer than you think.

The power of being grounded

Your root chakra is key to your ability to manifest. It is your foundation, the source of your stability, safety and sense of belonging. When your root chakra is open, you feel grounded, secure and confident, trusting deeply in the manifestation process. But when it is blocked, doubts and fears can hold you back, making it difficult to fully believe in your dreams. An open root chakra gives you the strength to pursue your goals with a sense of inner security, knowing you are supported and capable. When you feel grounded, manifestation becomes not just possible, but natural.

Worksheet 15: Manifestation with the root chakra worksheet for building a strong foundation

Write down, "Today, I nurture my dreams by creating a stable foundation within myself. As I connect with the energy of my root chakra, I feel grounded, secure and open to receiving. I trust that I have everything I need to build the life I desire. My journey is supported, and I walk forward with confidence. I am grateful for the stability and strength I am building in my life."

Affirmations for manifesting abundance with a solid foundation

- "I am a powerful creator of my dreams, grounded in my own strength."

- "I feel safe, secure and stable, welcoming abundance into my life."

- "My foundation is solid, and I am open to receiving all that I deserve."

Exercise 15.1: Clarify your goal and set your intention

- Write a clear and specific manifestation statement: Start by defining your goal very specifically. Ask yourself: *What do I truly want? Why do I want it? How will it positively affect my life?*

- Write your goal in the present tense and ensure it feels authentic to you. For example, "I am manifesting financial abundance to support my personal growth and future security."

- Keep this statement visible throughout the day as a reminder of your focus.

- Why this works? Clarity is essential in manifestation. The clearer your goal, the stronger your signal to the universe.

What do you truly want?

....

....

....

....

....

....

....

....

....

....

Why is it important in your life right now?

....

....

....

....

....

....

....

....

....

....

Manifestation and the beej mantra meditation for the root chakra

The root chakra is about stability, grounding and feeling secure in life, representing your foundation—home, health and basic needs. This meditation helps you tap into a deep sense of security, making you feel rooted and connected to the earth. Focusing on your root chakra strengthens your foundation, helping you feel supported and safe. Chanting the mantra "Lam" enhances this connection, aligning you with the energy of stability and balance.

- Find a quiet, comfortable space and close your eyes. Take a deep breath in and slowly release any tension, letting go of the stresses of your day. Focus on your breath, feeling each inhale bring calm, and each exhale release any negativity.

- Begin to silently repeat the mantra "Lam", allowing it to anchor you into the present moment. Picture a warm, red light glowing at the base of your spine, the colour of strength, stability and safety. With each breath, feel this light growing brighter, expanding and radiating throughout your entire body. Visualize it as a warm, healing energy that infuses you with grounding power, filling you with a deep sense of security.

- Now, shift your focus to the life you want to create. Visualize your ideal home—a place where you feel completely safe and at peace. See yourself surrounded by the security you need—whether it is health, financial stability or emotional support. Picture this energy filling your space, your body and your life, as the bright red light of the root chakra empowers your manifestation.

- Repeat to yourself: "I am grounded, supported and safe. I attract stability and abundance into my life. My foundation is strong, and I am open to receiving everything I need."

- Take a few more deep breaths, feeling the power of your root chakra fully activated within you. Gently move your fingers and toes, returning to the present moment. Notice how centred and thankful you feel. Trust that your connection with the root chakra is guiding you towards your desires, and carry that sense of trust and gratitude with you today, knowing you are aligned with your deepest needs and ready to receive the stability and abundance meant for you.

Yoga for the root chakra: Manifest your energy

Begin your day with a mindful flow to activate your root chakra, inviting stability, security and a deep sense of grounding.

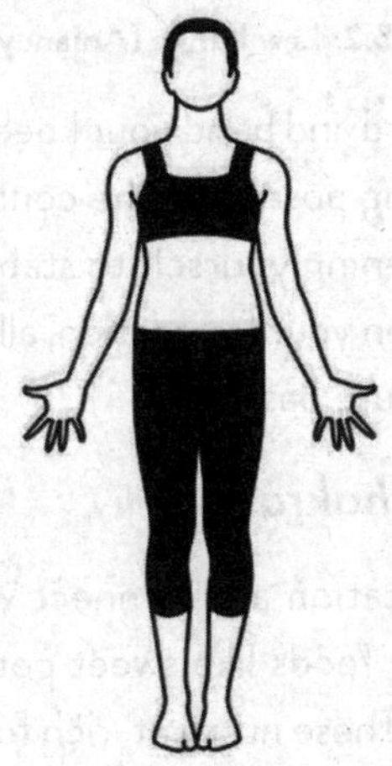

Asana 15.1: Mountain Pose (Tadasana)

Stand tall and rooted, feeling your feet connect firmly to the earth. Engage your legs and core, drawing energy from the ground, and establish a sense of balance and strength within. Let your breath flow deeply, grounding you in the present moment.

Asana 15.2: Low Lunge (Anjaneyasana)

Step one foot forward and bend your knee, grounding your back leg. As you sink into the pose, feel the connection between your feet and the earth, opening yourself to stability and support. This posture helps strengthen your foundation, allowing you to manifest your desires with a secure base.

Food for the root chakra

Support your manifestation and connect with your root chakra by choosing grounding foods like sweet potatoes, carrots, beets, quinoa and brown rice. These nutrient-rich foods promote stability, vitality and balance, helping you feel secure and aligned with the earth's energy. Sweet potatoes and beets provide physical grounding, while grains like quinoa and rice offer nourishment and steadiness. As you enjoy these foods, visualize them rooting you to the earth, supporting your goals and fostering abundance. With each bite, embrace the strength and stability that come from being grounded in your own foundation.

Exercise 15.2: Grounding and journaling

Start by heading outdoors to connect with nature. Walk barefoot on the grass or spend time in a quiet natural setting. As you walk, focus on grounding yourself, feeling the earth beneath your feet, and clearing your mind. Visualize your desires flowing into reality with each step. Let the energy of nature help you release any mental clutter and bring clarity to your goals.

Once you feel centred, sit down and begin your manifestation journaling. Reflect on what truly matters to you, clarifying your vision and goals. This process helps align your root chakra, creating a sense of stability and safety as you embrace your manifestation journey.

What are your short and long-term goals, both big and small?

What steps can you take today to move closer to these goals?

....

....

....

....

....

....

....

....

What obstacles or limiting beliefs are holding you back? How can you overcome them?

....

....

....

....

....

....

Closing Ritual: Reflect on manifestation and healing

As you complete Day 15, settle into a quiet space and take a moment to reflect on today's journey. Think about the actions, even the smallest steps, that moved you closer to your goals. Notice how each effort made you feel and how it aligns with your greater vision.

A promise to myself

Date:

Today, I took meaningful steps towards my dreams by ...

I am a powerful creator, manifesting my desires effortlessly.

Manifestation is a journey of grounding and growth. Now that you are aligned with your path, keep moving forward to create a life anchored in security, abundance and joy—for yourself and those around you. Trust in your foundation—you are building something deeply fulfilling.

Day 16 : Manifestation—release the old, embrace your dreams

> "When you let go of what's no longer serving you, you make space for what is meant for you."—Unknown

Sometimes, it feels like your life is shifting in amazing ways, like dreams are coming true before your eyes. That is the magic of manifestation. As you get clear on what you truly want, you will start attracting people who uplift and inspire you. Their energy supports your growth, making it feel like you are all on this journey together.

But with this clarity, you might also find yourself outgrowing certain relationships. It is like cleaning out an old closet—letting go of what no longer fits to make room for what does. While this can be difficult, it is a natural part of growth. Stay open, because new opportunities often come when you least expect them.

Celebrate each step forward, no matter how small. Aligning your thoughts, feelings and actions creates a powerful force that transforms your life in beautiful ways. Believe in yourself and take that leap. You are so close to the life you deserve—go get it.

Ignite passion

"What do we live for, if it is not to make life less difficult for each other?"—George Eliot

Your sacral chakra is deeply connected to creativity, passion and relationships—all essential for manifestation. When this chakra is open, you feel inspired, confident and connected to both yourself and others, allowing you to manifest with a sense of joy and purpose. Relationships become more harmonious, and you attract people who uplift and support your journey.

When the sacral chakra is blocked, however, self-doubt and emotional distance can creep in, making it hard to fully connect with your dreams or build fulfilling relationships. Trust in the power of this chakra to strengthen both your relationships and your vision. Let its energy inspire you. And watch as your dreams and connections, blossom.

Worksheet 16: Manifestation with the sacral worksheet for embracing creativity and joy

Write down, "Today, I allow my creativity to flow freely. I embrace my passions and desires, knowing they are a part of my true essence. I trust my intuition and let joy guide me as I manifest the life I deserve. I am open to experiencing life in its full expression, and I am grateful for the vibrant energy within me."

Affirmations for manifesting with creativity and passion

- "I am a creator of my own reality, filled with passion and creativity."

- "I trust my intuition and embrace the flow of life."

- "My desires are valid, and I welcome the joy that comes with them."

Exercise 16.1: Visualize your goal as already achieved

- Deep visualization practice: Now that you have set your intention on Day 16, spend 15–20 minutes visualizing your goal as already manifested. Close your eyes, relax and recall the goal you set. Imagine yourself living with the success of your manifestation.

- Engage all your senses in this experience—see, hear, feel, smell and taste it. Feel the emotions of already having it.

- End by saying, "Thank you, I am so grateful for this manifestation."

- Why this works: Visualization connects your mind and emotions to the desired outcome, making it feel real and attainable.

How does it feel to have already achieved your goal?

....

....

....

....

....

....

....

....

....

What are you doing, and who are you with in this vision?

....

....

....

....

....

....

....

....

Manifestation and beej mantra meditation for the sacral chakra

The sacral chakra is about creativity, emotions and relationships. It governs your connection to pleasure, passion and your ability to create. This meditation helps you unlock your creative potential, connecting you to the flow of your emotions and desires. Focusing on your sacral chakra empowers you to manifest healthy, vibrant relationships and creative abundance. Chanting the mantra "Vam" helps you align with the energy of creativity and emotional balance.

- Find a quiet, comfortable space, and close your eyes. Take a deep breath in and slowly release any tension, letting go of any emotional or physical strain. Focus on your breath, allowing each inhale to bring relaxation and each exhale to release any stagnant energy.

- Begin repeating the mantra silently "Vam", grounding you in the present moment. Picture a warm, orange light glowing in your lower abdomen, the colour of creativity, passion and connection. With each breath, feel this light growing stronger, expanding and filling you with creative energy, emotional balance and a deep sense of self-expression.

- Shift your focus to the life you wish to create. Visualize your relationships blossoming with love, harmony and understanding. Picture yourself radiating creativity and attracting what you desire with ease. See the energy of the sacral chakra infusing your life, your relationships and your dreams, making them vibrant and full of life.

- Repeat to yourself: "I am creative, passionate and connected. I attract love, joy and healthy relationships into my life. My emotional energy flows freely, and I am open to receiving all that nourishes my soul."

- Take a few more deep breaths, feeling the sacral chakra fully activated within you. Gently move your fingers and toes, returning to the present moment. Notice how aligned you feel with your desires, knowing that you are open to receiving the creative and emotional abundance that awaits you.

Yoga for the sacral chakra: Manifest your energy

Begin your day with a mindful flow to activate your sacral chakra, inviting emotional balance, creativity and connection to your desires.

Asana 16.1: Seated Forward Bend (Paschimottanasana)

Sit with your legs extended and fold forward, reaching for your toes. As you deepen into the stretch, feel the fluidity of your body and the opening of your hips. Let this movement release any emotional blockages, creating space for creative energy to flow freely.

Asana 16.2: Bound Angle Pose (Baddha Konasana)

Bring the soles of your feet together, gently pressing your knees towards the floor. Open your hips and allow your breath to guide you into a deeper connection with your sacral chakra. As you breathe into your pelvis, feel the flow of creativity, passion and emotional healing manifesting.

Food for the sacral chakra

Support your creative manifestation by choosing foods that ignite passion and emotional flow. Sweet fruits like oranges, mangoes and peaches, along with healthy fats from nuts and seeds, fuel your sacral chakra, encouraging vitality and creativity.

Oranges and mangoes are rich in vitamins and enzymes that promote emotional balance and joy. Nuts and seeds provide nourishing fats that help foster emotional stability. As you enjoy these foods, imagine them nurturing your creativity, bringing your desires to life. With each mindful bite, feel your emotional and creative energy flow freely, empowering your manifestation.

Exercise 16.2: Vision board

A vision board helps you visually manifest your dreams by keeping your goals in clear view. Start by gathering materials—magazines, images and a blank board, or create a digital version. Choose images, quotes or symbols that truly resonate with your desires. Arrange them on your board in a way that feels right, grouping by themes if desired, and personalize with affirmations or photos. Place your board somewhere you will see it daily, like your bedroom or workspace, and spend a few minutes each day visualizing and feeling the emotions connected to your goals. Update it as your goals evolve.

What images on your vision board resonate with you the most?

How do you envision your ideal life once you achieve these goals?

What are your core values?

How do your core values align with your goals?

... ...

... ...

Closing ritual: Reflect on manifestation and healing

As you complete Day 16, settle into a quiet space and take a moment to reflect on today's journey. Think about the actions, even the smallest steps, that moved you closer to your goals. Notice how each effort made you feel and how it aligns with your greater vision.

A promise to myself

Date:

Today, I took meaningful steps towards my dreams by ...

... ...

... ...

... ...

... ...

... ...

... ...

... ...

... ...

I embrace the abundance in my life and welcome joy and creativity.

Allow yourself to feel the full power of your desires. Embrace the pleasure of creating and manifesting from a place of joy and harmony. You are cultivating a life of deep connection and fulfilment.

Day 17 : Manifestation—harness the power of belief

"Positive anything is better than negative nothing."
—Elbert Hubbard

Have you ever noticed how your mindset shapes your reality? It is all part of the Law of Attraction, which is closely connected to manifestation. When you focus on positivity and abundance, you attract those same energies into your life. What you believe and think matters deeply because it influences what you draw in. This reminds us that our internal state creates our external world.

This idea ties closely to the concept of the "self-fulfilling prophecy". When you believe in your success, you are more likely to take the steps that lead to it. Your beliefs shape your actions, and in turn, your reality. Research shows that a positive mindset isn't just wishful thinking—it leads to real results.

Think of Oprah Winfrey, Mahendra Singh Dhoni, and many other successful people. They visualized their success long before it happened. Oprah imagined her path to greatness, and Dhoni envisioned victory before every match. Their belief and hard work turned their dreams into reality. You, too, have the power to shape your life. Trust in yourself, believe in your dreams and watch them come true.

Unlock your inner strength

Your solar plexus chakra is the centre of your personal power, confidence and will. When it is open, you feel strong, motivated and ready to take action on your dreams. You trust yourself and the manifestation process, knowing you have the strength to create the life you want. But when it is blocked, doubt, fear and insecurity can hold you back, making it harder to believe in your abilities. You may struggle to take inspired action or fully believe in your goals. Trust that when this chakra is balanced, your manifestations flow with ease and confidence. You are capable, powerful and deserving of everything you desire.

Worksheet 17: Manifestation with the solar plexus chakra worksheet for stepping into personal power

Write down, "Today, I step into my personal power with confidence. I trust in my abilities and stand strong in my worth. I am worthy of all the success and happiness I desire. My actions align with my purpose, and I am proud of the person I am becoming."

Affirmations for manifesting personal power and confidence

- "I am confident, capable and worthy of success."

- "I trust in my abilities and take bold action."

- "I am aligned with my purpose, and I attract the success I deserve."

Exercise 17.1: Release limiting beliefs and negative emotions

- Identify and transform limiting beliefs: Reflect on any fears, doubts or limiting beliefs that might be holding you back from manifesting your goal. Write down any negative thoughts you have about it.

- For each belief, create a counter statement that empowers you and aligns with your goal. For example, If you think, "I'm not good enough to have this", replace it with, "I am worthy of receiving all the abundance I desire."

- Repeat these affirmations throughout the day.

- Why this works: Limiting beliefs create resistance. Replacing them with positive beliefs clears the path to your goal and removes internal blocks.

What negative beliefs or fears have you been holding on to?

……

……

……

……

……

……

... ...

... ...

How can you reframe them to empower your manifestation?

... ...

... ...

... ...

... ...

... ...

... ...

... ...

... ...

Manifestation and beej mantra meditation for the solar plexus chakra

The solar plexus chakra is about confidence, personal power and taking action. It governs your sense of self, your willpower and your ability to manifest your goals. This meditation helps you step into your personal strength, allowing you to confidently pursue your dreams. Focusing on your solar plexus chakra amplifies your willpower and brings clarity to your goals. Chanting the mantra "Ram" connects you with the energy of self-esteem and inner strength.

Find a quiet, comfortable space and close your eyes. Take a deep breath in and slowly release any tension, letting go of self-doubt and uncertainty. Pay attention to your breathing, allowing each breath to offer clarity and each exhale to let go of any restricting thoughts.

- Silently repeat the mantra "Ram", grounding you in your inner strength. Visualize a bright, yellow light glowing in your solar plexus—the colour of confidence, power and purpose. With each breath, feel this light growing brighter and expanding, radiating strength, clarity, and self-assurance throughout your entire being.

- Shift your focus to the life you want to create. Visualize yourself taking confident steps towards your goals. See your dreams unfolding before you, empowered by your own will and strength. Feel your solar plexus chakra fuelling your personal power, helping you manifest the life you desire.

- Repeat to yourself: "I am confident, strong and capable. I attract success and personal power into my life. I trust my decisions, and I am open to receiving all that I deserve."

- Take a few more deep breaths, feeling the solar plexus chakra fully activated within you. Gently move your fingers and toes, returning to the present moment. Notice how empowered and focused you feel, knowing you are aligned with your desires and ready to take inspired action towards them.

Yoga for the solar plexus chakra: Manifest your energy

Begin your day with a mindful flow to activate your solar plexus chakra, inviting confidence, strength and personal power.

Asana 17.1: Warrior II (Virabhadrasana II)

Stand strong with your legs wide apart, arms extended and gaze forward. As you ground yourself in this powerful stance, feel the confidence and determination rising within. This posture activates your core and builds the strength needed to manifest your goals with purpose and clarity.

Asana 17.2: Boat Pose (Navasana)

Sit with your legs extended and lift your feet off the ground, balancing on your sit bones. As you hold this pose, feel the fire in your core, the seat of your personal power. Allow this strength to ignite your willpower, pushing you towards your manifestations with confidence and determination.

Food for the solar plexus chakra

Support your manifestation by choosing foods that promote strength, confidence and vitality. Whole grains like brown rice, oats and corn, along with yellow foods like bananas and lemons, nourish the solar plexus chakra, boosting your personal power and energy.

Bananas and lemons are full of energizing nutrients that support digestion and promote vitality. Whole grains fuel your body with sustained energy, helping you stay focused and confident. As you enjoy these foods, feel your personal power grow, empowering you to confidently manifest your dreams.

Exercise 17.2: 369 method

The 369 manifestation method uses the power of numbers and repetition to focus on your desire. Take a notebook or a diary and write your affirmation three times in the morning, six times in the afternoon and nine times at night. Choose a specific affirmation in the present tense, like "I am attracting financial prosperity effortlessly". Repeat this daily for 21 days, feeling the emotions as if your desire has already come true. This practice embeds your intention in your subconscious, strengthening your belief and helping to manifest your goal. The repetition and emotional engagement align you with your desire and keep your focus steady.

Closing ritual: Reflect on manifestation and healing

As you complete Day 17, settle into a quiet space and take a moment to reflect on today's journey. Think about the actions, even the smallest steps, that moved you closer to your goals. Notice how each effort made you feel and how it aligns with your greater vision.

A promise to myself

Date:

Today, I took meaningful steps towards my dreams by...

....

....

....

....

....

....

....

....

....

I embrace my inner strength and celebrate the abundance in my life.

Trust the fire within. Each step you take is guided by your strength and determination. Manifestation flows from your willingness to embrace your power and act boldly.

Day 18 : Manifestation—the power of accountability

"The future belongs to those who believe in the beauty of their dreams."—Eleanor Roosevelt

Ever feel like your dreams are just ... dreams? Sharing them with someone you trust can change everything. When you talk about your goals, they become real—like promises you are ready to keep. Accountability is powerful. Having an accountability partner or mentor can remind you of your goals when you are drifting.

When you focus, things start falling into place. That is manifestation—not magic, but clarity and intention. The more you commit, the more your dreams begin to unfold.

Don't be afraid to share your journey. Trust that your dreams are within reach, and with the right support, they will take shape. Keep believing and moving forward—every step brings you closer to your purpose. Imagine the clarity and focus you need to make your dreams reality. It is already inside you. Believe in yourself, and watch the magic happen. Taking control of your life is anything but easy. But you have got this!

Clear heart, clear path

When your heart chakra is open, you feel love, joy and compassion. It is like a magnet, attracting everything you truly desire. Manifestation flows effortlessly because you are aligned with your true self. You radiate positivity, making space for abundance and happiness.

But when it is blocked, fear, doubt or unworthiness can take over. Manifestation becomes harder because you are not fully open to receiving what life wants to offer. It feels like a wall between you and your dreams. Imagine a world where your heart is wide open and your desires flow freely. That is the power of a clear heart chakra, ready to manifest your best life. You deserve all the good things life has to offer. Believe in yourself and nurture your heart. When you do, everything starts falling into place. You have the power to create your reality. Let your heart lead the way.

Worksheet 18: Manifestation with the heart chakra worksheet for opening to love and compassion

Write down, "Today, I open my heart to receive and give love freely. I trust that the universe supports me in my journey of love, compassion and gratitude. I am worthy of all the love that is coming into my life, and I embrace it with an open heart."

Affirmations for manifesting love and compassion

- "I am open to love and I give love freely."
- "My heart is full of compassion and kindness."
- "I attract loving and fulfilling relationships into my life."

Exercise 18.1: Act with confidence and clarity

- Take aligned action: Today, commit to one tangible action that brings you closer to your goal. It could be a phone call, sending an email, researching opportunities or any action that aligns with your intention.

- As you take this step, trust that it is a powerful part of the manifestation process. Celebrate your action, no matter how small, as it moves you forward.

- Why this works: Action creates momentum and signals the universe that you are ready to receive your desires. It is a powerful step towards manifesting your goal.

What step can you take today to move closer to your manifestation?

………………………………………………………………………………………………………

………………………………………………………………………………………………………

………………………………………………………………………………………………………

………………………………………………………………………………………………………

………………………………………………………………………………………………………

………………………………………………………………………………………………………

………………………………………………………………………………………………………

………………………………………………………………………………………………………

How will this action feel when you take it?

………………………………………………………………………………………………………

………………………………………………………………………………………………………

………………………………………………………………………………………………………

………………………………………………………………………………………………………

………………………………………………………………………………………………………

… …

… …

… …

… …

Manifestation and beej mantra meditation for the heart chakra

The heart chakra is about love, compassion and healing. It governs your capacity to give and receive love, both from yourself and others. This meditation helps you open your heart to unconditional love and healing, creating space for more love to flow into your life. Focusing on your heart chakra encourages you to manifest love, peace and connection. Chanting the mantra "Yam" opens you to the energy of compassion and empathy.

- Find a quiet, comfortable space and close your eyes. Take a deep breath in and slowly release any tension, letting go of any emotional blockages. Focus on your breath, feeling each inhale bring love and each exhale release any heartache or resentment.

- Silently repeat the mantra "Yam", anchoring you in the present moment. Visualize a glowing, green light at the centre of your chest, the colour of love, compassion and healing. With each breath, feel this light growing brighter, radiating warmth, kindness and unconditional love throughout your entire body.

- Shift your focus to the love you want to create. Visualize yourself surrounded by loving, supportive relationships.

See love flowing freely between you and others, creating harmony, trust and deep connection. Feel the energy of the heart chakra healing and expanding your capacity for love and compassion.

- Repeat to yourself: "I am love, I am open to love and I am worthy of love. I attract loving, nurturing relationships into my life. My heart is open, and I am ready to receive love in all its forms."

- Take a few more deep breaths, feeling the heart chakra fully activated within you. Gently move your fingers and toes, returning to the present moment. Notice how peaceful and loving you feel, knowing that you are aligned with the love and connection you deserve.

Yoga for the heart chakra: Manifest your energy

Begin your day with a mindful flow to activate your heart chakra, inviting love, compassion and emotional openness.

Asana 18.1: Camel Pose (Ustrasana)

Kneel and gently arch your back, reaching your hands towards your feet. Open your chest and heart, allowing the energy of love to flow freely. This posture encourages emotional openness, helping you embrace both giving and receiving love, and creating space for love-based manifestation.

Asana 18.2: Child's Pose (Balasana)

Kneel and gently rest your forehead on the ground, extending your arms forward. As you relax into the pose, focus on opening your heart and inviting peace and love into your life. Feel the deep nurturing energy of your heart chakra, supporting your manifestation of love and compassion.

Food for the heart chakra

Support your manifestation by choosing foods that promote emotional healing and love. Green foods like spinach, kale and avocados, along with heart-healthy fats like olive oil and almonds, nourish the heart chakra, encouraging love and compassion.

Spinach and kale provide vitamins that support emotional balance, while avocados and olive oil offer healthy fats to promote overall well-being. As you enjoy these foods, imagine them nurturing your heart, inviting love and healing. With each mindful bite, feel your heart expand, empowering your manifestation of love.

Exercise 18.1: Glass bottle

The glass bottle manifestation method combines scent and visualization to keep your goals in focus. Write your specific desires on sticky notes in the present tense, as if they have already come true (for example, "I am grateful to be surrounded by loving relationships and fulfilling opportunities. My heart is full, and I am living my best life."). Fold the notes, place them in a small glass bottle and add a few drops of an uplifting essential oil, like lavender. Keep the bottle nearby, letting the scent serve as a daily reminder of your intentions. When you need motivation, inhale the aroma to reconnect with the positive emotions tied to your dreams.

Do you believe your desires are achievable?

....

....

....

....

....

....

....

....

....

What time-wasting habits have you had in the past that you will avoid now to achieve your goals?

………………………………………………………………………………………………………

………………………………………………………………………………………………………

………………………………………………………………………………………………………

………………………………………………………………………………………………………

………………………………………………………………………………………………………

………………………………………………………………………………………………………

………………………………………………………………………………………………………

………………………………………………………………………………………………………

………………………………………………………………………………………………………

Closing ritual: Reflect on manifestation and healing

As you complete Day 18, settle into a quiet space and take a moment to reflect on today's journey. Think about the actions, even the smallest steps, that moved you closer to your goals. Notice how each effort made you feel and how it aligns with your greater vision.

A promise to myself

Date:

Today, I took meaningful steps towards my dreams by …

………………………………………………………………………………………………………

………………………………………………………………………………………………………

… …

… …

… …

… …

… …

… …

… …

… …

I trust the power of my heart and the universe. I am manifesting my desires effortlessly, and I am open to receiving the love, abundance and joy that are already flowing to me.

Keep your heart open to the possibilities ahead. Manifesting from love brings abundance and harmony, attracting everything aligned with your highest good.

Day 19 : Manifestation—visualize, believe, achieve

"Victory is sweetest when you have known defeat."
—Malcolm Forbes

Have you ever had a dream so vivid that it felt like it was already yours? That is the magic of manifestation. It starts with a clear vision of what you truly desire. Close your eyes, feel it in your heart and believe—truly believe—that it is already yours. You deserve it. Now, take action, no matter how small. Every step you take brings you closer to making that dream a reality. *Trust in the process and in yourself.* The universe is listening, and with each move, you are one step closer to the life you have always imagined.

Let go of fears and doubts, and replace them with belief in your worth. Manifestation is about more than just wishing—it is about taking inspired steps towards the life you want. Stay patient, stay grateful and enjoy the journey. Celebrate the small wins because they all lead to something bigger. When you acknowledge your wins, you are essentially acknowledging your worth.

You are capable of amazing things, and the life you dream of is waiting for you. Keep going, and believe in yourself. Your dreams are already on their way. You have got this!

Express yourself, embrace your dreams

Have you ever felt like your dreams just wouldn't come true, no matter how hard you tried? It might be because your throat chakra, the centre of communication and self-expression, is blocked. When this happens, it is like a tap is shut off—your desires are there, but they can't flow into the world. You may struggle to speak your truth, feeling unheard or unsure of yourself.

But when your throat chakra is open your words will have power, and your desires manifest effortlessly. You believe in yourself and your ability to create the life you want. You express your truth boldly, aligning with your authentic self. Isn't it worth unlocking your potential and manifesting everything you have ever dreamed of?

Worksheet 19: Manifest with the throat chakra worksheet for speaking your truth

Write down, "Today, I speak my truth with confidence and clarity. I trust that my voice is powerful and that my words create the reality I desire. I am unapologetically authentic, and I embrace my right to be heard."

Affirmations for manifesting clarity and authenticity

- "I speak my truth with courage and clarity."
- "My voice is powerful, and my words create my reality."
- "I trust that my authenticity leads me to the life I deserve."

Exercise 19.1: Focus on gratitude and raise your vibration

- Gratitude practice: Begin the day by listing five things you are grateful for. These can be related to your goal or anything that brings you joy.

- Throughout the day, repeat gratitude affirmations like, "I am so grateful for the abundance in my life", or "I am thankful for the opportunities that are opening for me".

- Gratitude raises your vibration and makes it easier to attract what you want.

- Why this works: Gratitude shifts your energy to a higher frequency, aligning you with abundance and making manifestation easier.

What are the five things you are grateful for today?

....

....

....

....

....

... ...

... ...

... ...

... ...

... ...

How does gratitude help you feel more aligned with your goal?

... ...

... ...

... ...

... ...

... ...

... ...

... ...

... ...

Manifestation and beej mantra meditation for the throat chakra

The throat chakra is about communication, self-expression and authenticity. It governs your ability to speak your truth and express yourself freely. This meditation helps you find your authentic voice, empowering you to communicate your needs and desires. Focusing on your throat chakra enhances your self-expression and supports your ability to manifest your truth. Chanting the mantra "Ham" helps you align with the energy of clear communication and authenticity.

- Find a quiet, comfortable space and close your eyes. Take a deep breath in and slowly release any tension, letting go of any fears or doubts about speaking your truth. Focus on your breath, feeling each inhale bring clarity and each exhale release any barriers to authentic self-expression.

- Silently repeat the mantra "Ham", grounding you in your voice and personal truth. Visualize a blue light glowing at your throat, the colour of communication, clarity and expression. With each breath, feel this light growing brighter and expanding, empowering your voice and helping you speak with confidence and authenticity.

- Shift your focus to the life you want to create. Visualize yourself expressing your desires clearly and confidently, knowing that your voice has the power to manifest your reality. See yourself being heard and understood, with your words aligning with your inner truth.

- Repeat to yourself: "I speak my truth with confidence and clarity. I attract opportunities to express myself authentically. My voice is powerful and I am open to receiving all that I deserve." Take a few more deep breaths, feeling the throat chakra fully activated within you. Gently move your fingers and toes, returning to the present moment. Notice how empowered and clear-headed you feel, knowing you are aligned with your authentic voice and ready to manifest your truth.

Yoga for the throat chakra: Manifest your energy

Begin your day with a mindful flow to activate your throat chakra, inviting clear communication, self-expression, and truth.

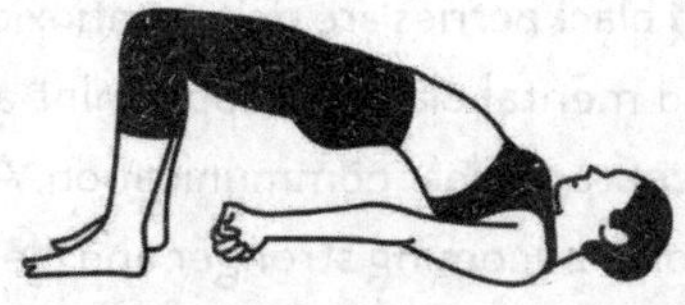

Asana 19.1: Bridge Pose (Setu Bandhasana)

Lie on your back with your knees bent and feet flat on the floor, lifting your hips towards the sky. As you lift your chest, open your throat and jaw, allowing your voice to be free. This posture stimulates the throat chakra, helping you express your truth clearly and confidently.

Asana 19.2: Fish Pose (Matsyasana)

Lie on your back, arch your chest upwards and gently rest the crown of your head on the floor. Open your throat, inviting clear expression and authentic communication. This pose supports the flow of energy through the throat chakra, aligning you with your truth.

Food for the throat chakra

Support your manifestation by choosing foods that promote clarity of speech and self-expression. Blue foods like blueberries, blackberries and grapes, along with soothing herbs like peppermint and ginger, nourish the throat chakra, promoting clear and confident communication.

Blueberries and blackberries are rich in antioxidants that support brain function and mental clarity. Peppermint and ginger soothe the throat and encourage clear communication. As you enjoy these foods, feel your voice becoming stronger and clearer, empowering you to manifest with authenticity and truth.

Exercise 19.2: Accountability partner and award speech

Write an award speech as if you have already achieved your goal, imagining you are being honoured for it. Stand on stage in your mind, feeling pride, gratitude and accomplishment. Then, if possible, share this speech with a friend or mentor who can keep you accountable. Afterwards, deliver it confidently in front of a mirror, fully embracing the emotions of success.

How to Write: Use the present tense, describing your accomplishments and feelings with specificity, like: "I'm so grateful for this award recognizing my journey as a successful entrepreneur. The challenges were worth it, and the support from my loved ones made it all possible."

I am so grateful for this award recognizing my ...

… …

… …

....

....

....

....

....

....

....

Do I feel more motivated after sharing my goals?

....

....

....

....

....

....

....

....

Closing ritual: Reflect on manifestation and healing

As you complete Day 19, settle into a quiet space and take a moment to reflect on today's journey. Think about the actions, even the smallest steps, that moved you closer to your goals. Notice how each effort made you feel and how it aligns with your greater vision.

A promise to myself

Date:

Today, I took meaningful steps towards my dreams by ...

....

....

....

....

....

....

....

....

....

I trust the power of my voice and the universe. I am manifesting my desires effortlessly and speaking my dreams into existence.

Each word and thought has power. Manifest your vision by communicating with honesty and openness, knowing that your authentic voice leads the way.

Day 20 : Manifestation—begins in the mind

> "The mind is not a vessel to be filled, but a fire to
> be kindled."—Plutarch

Your mind is a powerful tool. When you visualize your dreams, you are not just imagining—you are actively shaping your reality. By focusing on what you want, you send a clear message to your brain that your goals are possible. It responds by releasing feel-good chemicals, boosting your motivation and helping you take the steps to bring those dreams to life.

When you visualize success, your brain starts to see opportunities, not obstacles. It boosts your confidence and aligns your thoughts with your dreams. The key areas of your brain light up, helping you make decisions, feel joy and stay motivated. Visualization and affirmations create a mental space that nurtures your desires, empowering you to turn your dreams into reality.

Keep visualizing, keep believing in yourself and trust that your dreams are already on their way. You are capable, and everything you want is within reach. Keep moving forward; your future is waiting for you.

Clear sight, clear path

Manifestation and your third eye chakra are deeply connected. When your third eye is open, you have clarity and insight, allowing your dreams and goals to flow with ease. You see opportunities clearly and trust your intuition to guide you. But when blocked, doubts, confusion and a lack of vision can hold you back. You may struggle to see the path forward, feeling stuck. Unblocking your third eye brings a sense of empowerment and purpose, helping you manifest your desires with confidence and trust. Remember, when your vision is clear, the universe will align to support you.

Worksheet 20: Manifestation with the third eye chakra worksheet for trusting your intuition

Write down, "Today, I trust my intuition and allow it to guide me. I am connected to the wisdom within me, and I trust that the answers I seek are already inside me. I am open to receiving insights that lead me towards my dreams."

Affirmations for manifesting clarity and intuition

- "I trust my inner wisdom and guidance."

- "I am connected to my intuition, and it leads me toward my desires."

- "I am open to receiving the insights and clarity I need to manifest my dreams."

Exercise 20.1: Detach and trust the process

- Let go and trust: Spend 10–15 minutes meditating on detaching from the outcome. Sit quietly, breathe deeply and focus on releasing control. Trust that you have already set your intention, visualized it, taken action and now it is time to let go and allow the universe to deliver.

- Remind yourself that everything is unfolding perfectly in its own time.
- Why this works: Detaching allows the manifestation to flow naturally without resistance. Trusting the process creates space for the universe to work its magic.

How can you release what you are trying to control and trust in the process?

....

....

....

....

....

....

....

....

Manifestation and beej mantra meditation for the third eye chakra

The third eye chakra is about intuition, insight and vision. It governs your ability to see beyond the physical world and connect with your inner wisdom. This meditation helps you strengthen your intuition, guiding you to trust your inner knowing. Focusing on your third eye chakra enhances your clarity, vision and ability to manifest your desires with spiritual insight. Chanting the mantra "Om" connects you to the energy of perception and higher understanding.

Find a quiet, comfortable space and close your eyes. Take a deep breath in, and slowly release any tension, letting go of doubt and confusion. Focus on your breath, feeling each inhale bring clarity and each exhale release mental fog.

- Silently repeat the mantra "Om", grounding you in higher wisdom. Visualize an indigo light glowing between your eyebrows, the colour of intuition, insight and spiritual vision. With each breath, feel this light growing brighter and expanding, awakening your inner sight and helping you connect with your higher self.

- Shift your focus to the life you want to create. Visualize your goals with clarity, seeing them unfold with precision and ease. Trust your intuition to guide you towards your desires, and see your path illuminated by the light of your third eye.

- Repeat to yourself: "I trust my intuition, and I see my path clearly. I attract clarity, vision and guidance into my life. My mind is open to receiving insight and wisdom."

- Take a few more deep breaths, feeling the third eye chakra fully activated within you. Gently move your fingers and toes, returning to the present moment. Notice how clear-headed and confident you feel, knowing that you are aligned with your intuition and ready to manifest your deepest desires.

Yoga for the third eye chakra: Manifest your energy

Begin your day with a mindful flow to activate your third eye chakra, inviting clarity, intuition and inner wisdom.

Asana 20.1: Downward-Facing Dog (Adho Mukha Svanasana)

Start in a plank position, then lift your hips towards the sky, forming an inverted V. As you press your hands into the ground and your heels towards the floor, let your mind open to new insights and intuitive wisdom. This posture activates the third eye, sharpening your awareness and guiding your manifestation process.

Asana 20.2: Child's Pose (Balasana)

Kneel and rest your forehead on the floor. Allow your mind to quiet down, focusing on the space between your eyebrows. This posture invites deep inner knowing, helping you connect with your intuition and receive guidance for your manifestations.

Food for the third eye chakra

Support your manifestation by choosing foods that enhance intuition and mental clarity. Purple foods like eggplant, grapes and purple potatoes, along with dark chocolate and nuts, nourish the third eye chakra, inviting inner wisdom and spiritual insight.

Eggplants and purple potatoes are full of antioxidants that support brain health, while dark chocolate offers clarity and focus. Dark chocolate contains natural compounds like caffeine, theobromine, and flavonoids that can enhance focus, improve blood flow to the brain, and lift the mood, supporting clarity and mental alertness in subtle but effective ways.

Nuts provide healthy fats that nourish your mind, supporting your intuition. As you savour these foods, feel your intuition strengthening, empowering your manifestation process.

Exercise 20.2: Empty chair

Sit across from an empty chair in a quiet space, imagining your future, successful self-sitting there. Begin an interview: ask how you achieved your dreams, overcame obstacles and adopted a success-focused mindset. Listen closely, then switch chairs and embody your future self, responding with advice and encouragement as if you have already achieved your goals.

Afterwards, sit quietly, focusing on your third eye chakra. Visualize a calming indigo light filling your mind, enhancing your intuition and clarity. Let the feeling of accomplishment settle within you, amplifying your focus and manifestation energy.

What did your future self share about the key steps to achieving your dreams?

What qualities did your future self-embody that you admire?

What message did your future self have for you?

....

....

....

....

....

....

....

....

....

....

Closing ritual: Reflect on manifestation and healing

As you complete Day 20, settle into a quiet space and take a moment to reflect on today's journey. Think about the actions, even the smallest steps, that moved you closer to your goals. Notice how each effort made you feel and how it aligns with your greater vision.

A promise to myself

Date:

Today, I took meaningful steps towards my dreams by ...

... ...

... ...

... ...

... ...

... ...

... ...

... ...

... ...

... ...

... ...

I trust the power of my vision and intuition. I am manifesting my desires effortlessly, and I see my dreams becoming reality.

Clarity comes from within. As you visualize your dreams, let your inner sight illuminate the way. Manifestation is empowered by your intuitive knowing and spiritual awareness.

Day 21 : Manifestation—discover the magic within you

"The universe responds to the vibrational frequency of your thoughts and feelings."—Rhonda Byrne

I have always dreamed of building a career I truly loved. As I visualized each step, doors began to open. *Manifestation isn't about wishing; it is about feeling as though you already have what you desire.* It is about trusting yourself and taking action. When you connect with your desires, they unfold naturally, empowering you to make choices that align with your heart, not others' expectations.

I remember dreaming of visiting Paris, imagining myself walking through the streets. Before I knew it, I was standing under the Eiffel Tower, filled with joy. That is the power of manifestation.

It is not just about getting what you want; it is about enjoying the journey, celebrating small victories and learning along the way. Opportunities often appear when you least expect them. By aligning your thoughts, emotions and actions, you create the energy to make your dreams a reality. *Trust the process.* Take the leap. You have the ability to shape your reality, and the world is waiting for you to embrace your potential. Keep going—your dreams are within reach.

Unlock the universe's flow

Your crown chakra connects you to the universe, aligning you with your true purpose. When it is open, you feel a deep sense of trust and know that everything you desire is already on its way. Manifestation flows naturally, and your dreams unfold with ease. But when it is blocked, doubt and confusion can cloud your vision, making you feel disconnected or stuck. This can slow down your manifestation. Embrace the power of your crown chakra. When it is balanced, you feel confident and supported by the universe. Trust this energy and watch how your dreams begin to take shape. You are deeply connected to your path, and everything you want is already coming to you.

Worksheet 21: Manifestation with the crown chakra worksheet for aligning with higher consciousness

Write down, "Today, I connect with the universe's infinite wisdom and guidance. I trust that I am aligned with my higher self and that I am exactly where I need to be. I am grateful for the clarity and understanding that I have gained on my journey."

Affirmations for manifesting alignment and universal guidance

- "I am connected to the universe and my higher self."

- "I trust in the divine guidance that leads me towards my desires."

- "I am aligned with abundance, love and higher consciousness."

Exercise 21.1: Reflect, celebrate and align with your future self

- Reflection and celebration: Reflect on the last six days. Write down any shifts or insights you have experienced. How have you changed? How has your energy aligned with your goal?

- End the day by celebrating your progress, whether with a treat, dance or moment of accomplishment.

- Why this works: Reflection and celebration amplify your manifestation energy, reinforcing your belief in what you are creating.

How have you changed over the last week?

…… …… …… …… …… …… …… …… …… …… …… …… …… …… …… …… …… …… …… ……

…… …… …… …… …… …… …… …… …… …… …… …… …… …… …… …… …… …… …… ……

…… …… …… …… …… …… …… …… …… …… …… …… …… …… …… …… …… …… …… ……

…… …… …… …… …… …… …… …… …… …… …… …… …… …… …… …… …… …… …… ……

…… …… …… …… …… …… …… …… …… …… …… …… …… …… …… …… …… …… …… ……

…… …… …… …… …… …… …… …… …… …… …… …… …… …… …… …… …… …… …… ……

…… …… …… …… …… …… …… …… …… …… …… …… …… …… …… …… …… …… …… ……

…… …… …… …… …… …… …… …… …… …… …… …… …… …… …… …… …… …… …… ……

…… …… …… …… …… …… …… …… …… …… …… …… …… …… …… …… …… …… …… ……

How does your energy align with the manifestation of your goal?

…… …… …… …… …… …… …… …… …… …… …… …… …… …… …… …… …… …… …… ……

…… …… …… …… …… …… …… …… …… …… …… …… …… …… …… …… …… …… …… ……

…… …… …… …… …… …… …… …… …… …… …… …… …… …… …… …… …… …… …… ……

…… …… …… …… …… …… …… …… …… …… …… …… …… …… …… …… …… …… …… ……

…… …… …… …… …… …… …… …… …… …… …… …… …… …… …… …… …… …… …… ……

Manifestation and beej mantra meditation for the crown chakra

The crown chakra is about connection, spirituality and higher consciousness. It governs your connection to the divine and your sense of purpose. This meditation helps you connect with your higher self, empowering you to align with your highest potential. Focusing on your crown chakra opens you to divine wisdom and guides you to manifest your spiritual and life goals. Chanting the mantra "Om" connects you to the energy of universal consciousness and spiritual alignment.

- Find a quiet, comfortable space and close your eyes. Take a deep breath in and slowly release any tension, letting go of any attachments or limitations. Focus on your breath, feeling each inhale bring spiritual connection and each exhale release any resistance.

- Silently repeat the mantra "Om", grounding you in divine consciousness. Visualize a violet light glowing at the top of your head, the colour of spirituality, enlightenment and divine connection. With each breath, feel this light growing brighter and expanding, opening your mind and soul to higher wisdom and universal energy.

- Shift your focus to the life you want to create. Visualize yourself aligned with your divine purpose, living in harmony with your highest calling. See your life filled with peace, wisdom and spiritual abundance, guided by the light of your crown chakra.

- Repeat to yourself: "I am connected to the divine and I trust in the flow of life. I attract spiritual wisdom, guidance and purpose into my life. I am open to receiving all that the universe has in store for me."

- Take a few more deep breaths, feeling the crown chakra fully activated within you. Gently move your fingers and toes, returning to the present moment. Notice how connected and peaceful you feel, knowing that you are aligned with your highest self and ready to manifest your spiritual and earthly desires.

Yoga for the crown chakra: Manifest your energy

Begin your day with a mindful flow to activate your crown chakra, inviting enlightenment, connection and spiritual growth.

Asana 21.1: Tree Pose (Vriksasana)

Stand tall with one foot grounded and the other foot placed on your inner thigh or calf. Bring your palms together above your head, reaching for the sky. This pose connects you to the earth while opening you to the divine, allowing your manifestation to align with your higher purpose.

Asana 21.2: Corpse Pose (Shavasana)

Lie down with your body fully relaxed and your palms facing up. Focus on the space above your head, inviting a sense of peace, oneness and connection with the universe. This posture helps align your energy with your highest self, inviting your deepest desires into manifestation.

Food for the crown chakra

Support your manifestation by choosing light, nourishing foods that enhance spiritual connection and inner clarity. Gentle options like coconut, cauliflower and small portions of white rice can help soothe the body and mind, supporting the crown chakra's energy. These foods promote a sense of peace, clarity and oneness with the universe, especially when enjoyed mindfully as part of your healing practice.

Coconut offers a calming effect, while cauliflower provides nutrients that support brain function and mental clarity. White rice offers light, easily digestible energy that helps you feel grounded and connected. As you savour these foods, visualize them aligning your energy with higher consciousness, gently guiding your manifestation towards spiritual fulfilment.

Exercise 21.2: Letter to your future self

Imagine yourself as the future you who has already achieved your dreams. Write a letter from this version of yourself to your present self, vividly describing what life is like now, how it feels to have reached your goal and the important steps you took along the way. Include any advice, encouragement and mindset shifts that made this success possible. As you write, fully engage with feelings of gratitude and pride. This exercise strengthens your focus, fuels belief in your vision and reinforces the energy of your manifestation, bringing you closer to your goal with each word.

....

....

....

....

....

....

....

....

....

Closing ritual: Reflect on manifestation and healing

As you complete this 21-day journey, take a quiet moment to celebrate how far you have come. Reflect on each action you have taken, each small step that has brought you closer to your dreams. Let yourself feel the pride, joy and strength that come from honouring your vision. Today, know that you are ready for all that lies ahead. Keep believing in your journey—the life you desire is unfolding right before you.

A promise to myself

Date:

Today, I honour the progress I have made and the strength I have shown in moving closer to my vision ...

....

....

....

....

....

....

....

....

....

I am connected to the universe, and I trust my higher self. My dreams are manifesting beautifully.

Take a moment to celebrate your efforts and acknowledge how far you have come. Feel the energy of your intentions aligning with your actions and notice the progress you have made.

Congratulations on completing this 21-day journey

Manifestation is a journey of growth and possibility, and today marks a powerful milestone. Trust in the path you have created—you are building a life of purpose, joy and abundance. Keep going; everything you have envisioned is within reach. Your commitment has laid a strong foundation, and now, the future you have dreamed of is ready for you.

9 ··—·· The End of One Chapter, the Beginning of a New You

"Your life does not get better by chance; it gets better by change."—Jim Rohn

Wow, you did it! Congratulations on completing this incredible 21-day journey of transformation. You have poured your heart and soul into healing your mind, body and spirit. The practices—forgiveness, gratitude, manifestation and chakra healing—are your powerful tools for a brighter future. Every little step you took, every moment of effort, has brought you closer to the peace, purpose and clarity you deserve.

You have learned that healing isn't just about fixing things, it is about letting go of the past, living fully in the present moment and opening yourself up to amazing new possibilities. You have rediscovered your inner strength and built a belief in your ability to change. Remember, it is not about being perfect, it is about making progress. Those small, consistent actions you took each day truly matter. They have made a lasting impact on your life.

Keep that momentum going and believe in your ability to achieve your goals. The wisdom and tools you have gained are not just for 21 days—they are for life. These practices will continue to guide you through any challenge. You have already proven to yourself that you can transform. Keep believing in yourself and your power to create the life you have always dreamed of. These exercises are your personal guide, ready whenever you need them.

"The only journey is the one within."
Rainer Maria Rilke

This is just the beginning. Continue on this journey of life, and healing is a part of that journey. *Keep healing, keep growing, keep moving forward.* The best version of you is within reach, waiting to be revealed. Your journey is a story; make each chapter count. You are worthy of all the peace, success and joy you desire. Your journey has just begun and the possibilities are endless. Keep going—you are stronger than you know, and your future is waiting for you.

What are your reflections on your journey?

"Never doubt the universe. You are one of a kind, and so is your journey. The strength within you is limitless—you can overcome any challenge. Just keep believing in yourself and trust that the best is yet to unfold."—Koutilya Chhajed

Bibliography

Books

Chopra, D. (2004). *The Seven Spiritual Laws of Success: A Practical Guide to the Fulfillment of Your Dreams*. Amber-Allen Publishing.

—(2015). *The Healing Self: A Revolutionary New Plan to Supercharge Your Immune System and Stay Well for Life*. Harmony Books.

—(2017). *The Seven Spiritual Laws of Success: A Practical Guide to the Fulfillment of Your Dreams* (revised edition). Amber-Allen Publishing.

Dyer, W.W. (2004). *The Power of Intention: Learning to Co-Create Your World Your Way*. Hay House.

Gawain, S. (1996). *Creative Visualization: Use the Power of Your Imagination to Create What You Want in Your Life*. New World Library.

Goleman, D. (1995). *Emotional Intelligence: Why It Can Matter More Than IQ*. Bantam Books.

—(2013). *Focus: The Hidden Driver of Excellence*. HarperCollins.

Hanson, R. (2018). *Hardwiring Happiness: The New Brain Science of Contentment, Calm, and Confidence*. Harmony Books.

Hargrave, T.D., and W.D. Pearson (2000). *Forgiveness: A Bold Choice for a Peaceful Heart*. Deseret Book Company.

Hendricks, G. (2010). *The Big Leap: Conquer Your Hidden Fear and Take Life to the Next Level*. Harper One.

Kabat-Zinn, J. (1990). *Full Catastrophe Living: Using the Wisdom of Your Body and Mind to Face Stress, Pain, and Illness*. Delta Trade Paperbacks.

—(2005). *Wherever You Go, There You Are: Mindfulness Meditation in Everyday Life*. Hyperion.

Neff, K. D. (2011). *Self-Compassion: The Proven Power of Being Kind to Yourself*. William Morrow.

Peters, S. (2016). *Yoga for Emotional Balance: Simple Practices to Help Relieve Anxiety and Depression*. Shambhala Publications.

Robbins, T. (1991). *Awaken the Giant Within: How to Take Immediate Control of Your Mental, Emotional, Physical, and Financial Destiny*. Free Press.

Siegel, D. J. (2010). *The Mindful Therapist: A Clinician's Guide to Mindsight and Neural Integration*. W.W. Norton & Company.

Tolle, E. (2004). *The Power of Now: A Guide to Spiritual Enlightenment*. New World Library.

—(2005). *A New Earth: Awakening to Your Life's Purpose*. Penguin Group.

Vasant, K. (2011). *The Chakra System: A Complete Course in Self-Diagnosis and Healing*. Llewellyn Worldwide.

Voss, C. (2016). *Never Split the Difference: Negotiating As If Your Life Depended On It*. Harper Business.

Whitelaw, J. (2015). *Chakra Healing: A Beginner's Guide to Self-Healing Techniques That Balance the Chakras*. Adams Media.

Young, P. (2021). *The Energy Codes: The 7-Step System to Awaken Your Spirit, Heal Your Body, and Live Your Best Life*. Hay House.

Zukav, G. (2000). *The Seat of the Soul: 25th Anniversary Edition*. Simon & Schuster.

Articles and Journals

Baker, L. (2019). "The Mind-Body connection: How Mental Health Affects Physical Health." *Journal of Health Psychology*, 24(8), pp. 1100–1112.

Brown, B. (2010). "The Power of Vulnerability." *Psychology Today*. https://www.psychologytoday.com/articles/the-power-of-vulnerability

Emmons, R.A., and M.E. McCullough (2003). "Counting Blessings versus Burdens: An Experimental Investigation of Gratitude and Subjective Well-Being in Daily Life." *Journal of Personality and Social Psychology*, 84(2), pp. 377–389.
https://doi.org/10.1037/0022-3514.84.2.377

Gartner, H. (2019). "How to Unblock Your Chakras: A Guide to Energetic Healing." Mind Body Green.
http://www.mindbodygreen.com/articles/how-to-unblock-chakras)

Gendler, T. (2017). "Visualizing your dreams: The science behind manifestation." Harvard Health Blog.
https://www.health.harvard.edu/articles/visualizing-manifestation

Jeong, S. (2018). "How Gratitude Can Help You Manifest Your Desires." *Psychology Today*.
https://www.psychologytoday.com/articles/how-gratitude-helps-manifest

Websites

Chopra Center. (n.d.). "Chakra Meditation and Healing."
https://www.chopra.com

Chopra Center. (2024). "Chakras: The Seven Energy Centers." Chopra.com.
https://www.chopra.com/articles/chakras-the-seven-energy-centers

Mayo Clinic. (2023). "How Energy Centers Affect Your Health."
http://www.mayoclinic.org/energy-centers-wellness

Mindful.org. (2021). "How to Create a Mindful Practice for Your Daily Life."
https://www.mindful.org

The Secret. (2023). "How the Law of Attraction Works."
https://www.thesecret.tv

Vuma Business. (2023, June 15). "A Lifetime at Work."
https://vumabusiness.com/2023/06/15/a-lifetime-at-work

Manage Business. (2023). "Employees Spend 30% of their Weekly Time at Work, Commuting, and Preparation." https://managebusiness.org/employees-spend-30-time-at-work

Total Jobs. (2018). UK Workers Will Spend over a Year of Their Lives Commuting. https://www.totaljobs.com/media-centre/uk-workers-will-spend-over-a-year-of-their-lives-commuting

Our World in Data. (2021). "How Do We Spend Our Time?" https://ourworldindata.org/time-use

National Sleep Foundation. (n.d.). "How Much Sleep Do We Really Need?" https://www.thensf.org

OECD Better Life Index. (2019). "Education." https://www.oecdbetterlifeindex.org/topics/education

U.S. Bureau of Labor Statistics (BLS). (2017). "Time Spent in Educational Activities in 2016." TED: The Economics Daily. https://www.bls.gov/opub/ted/2017/time-spent-in-ed-cational-activities-in-2016.htm

UN Statistics Division. (2016). "International Classification of Activities for Time-Use Statistics (ICATUS 2016)." https://unstats.un.org/unsd/demographic-social/time-use/icatus-2016/tableview

Wikipedia. (n.d.). "Informal Learning." https://en.wikipedia.org/wiki/Informal_learning

Reddit. (n.d.). "User-estimated \~630 days of Schooling (\~1.73 years) Spent in Education System (excluding college)." https://www.reddit.com/r/teenagers/comments/ykfsle

United Nations, Department of Economic and Social Affairs, Population Division. (2024). "World Population Prospects 2024." United Nations. https://population.un.org/wpp/

World Health Organization. (2022, June 17). "Mental Disorders."

https://www.who.int/news-room/fact-sheets/detail/mental-disorders

Our World in Data. (2023). "Global Average Life Expectancy has more than Doubled since 1900." https://ourworldindata.org/data-insights/global-average-life-expectancy-has-more-than-doubled-since-1900

Worldometer. (2025). "Life Expectancy of the World Population." https://www.worldometers.info/demographics/life-ex pectancy/

World Economic Forum. (2023, February). "How Life Expectancy is Changing around the World." https://www.weforum.org/stories/2023/02/charted-how-life-expectancy-is-changing-around-the-world/

Audiobooks

Goldstein, T. (2024). "Manifestation Mastery." Episode 24, "Aligned action: Making Your Manifestations a Reality." Available on Apple Podcasts and Spotify.

Hubbard, L. R. (1950). "Dianetics: The Modern Science of Mental Health." Bridge Publications.

Lambert, S. (2023). "Living the Dream: A Manifestation Journey." Episode 18, "Building Confidence in Your Manifestations." Available on Spotify and Google Podcasts.

Acknowledgements

This book has been as much a journey of healing as it has been an act of creation. Writing *The Ultimate Reboot* taught me that every expression is also a transformation. The process called for research and discipline, but just as much for surrender, patience and faith. In many ways, it mirrored the very path the book offers—moving through resistance, finding balance and opening to deeper truths.

A book is never born in isolation. It is shaped by voices, experiences, and encouragements that are not always visible. This work carries the wisdom I have been privileged to witness in my work with people—their stories, questions and courage to grow. Each encounter reminded me that healing is not solitary but a shared unfolding, and this book reflects that collective journey.

To my publisher, Ajay Mago, for believing in this book and its potential. Your support gave it not only a platform but also the reassurance that it was meant to reach those who might need it. Publishing is more than business—it is an act of trust in a writer's dream, and I am grateful you placed that trust in me.

I am deeply thankful to Shantanu Ray Chaudhuri, chief editor of Om Books International for seeing the seed of this work and nurturing it with conviction.

A heartfelt acknowledgment goes to my editor, Jyotsna Mehta. This book carries your quiet but lasting imprint. Your thoughtful feedback, steady encouragement and ability to sense the pulse of the manuscript made all the difference. You helped me discover its rhythm and ensured its essence remained intact. I could not have asked for a more compassionate and insightful guide on this journey.

To my parents, family and friends—you have been my anchor and my reminder of love. Your patience and quiet belief gave me the strength to move forward, even on the days when writing felt heavy. In many ways, this book is as much yours as it is mine.

To all those who have trusted me as clients, students or participants in workshops—you may not realize how deeply your journeys have become part of my own. Your courage to face pain, your openness to healing and your determination to grow have been my greatest inspiration. You have shown me, again and again, the extraordinary resilience within us all, and that forgiveness, though difficult, is always possible.

Finally, to the universe—thank you for conspiring in unseen ways to make this dream a reality. For the serendipitous meetings, the timely nudges, the moments of stillness and the bursts of clarity; I remain humbly grateful. This book is but a small offering back to the greater mystery that guides us all.